All of Grace

Other Titles by Charles Spurgeon

The Anointed Life

Being God's Friend

Evening by Evening

Finding Peace in Life's Storms

God Loves You

God Promises You

Grace and Power

Grace: God's Unmerited Favor

Holy Spirit Power

How to Have Real Joy

Joy in Christ's Presence

Joy in Your Life

Morning and Evening

Morning by Morning

The Power in Praising God

The Power in Prayer

Power in the Blood

Power over Satan

Prayer

Praying Successfully

The Soulwinner

Spiritual Parenting

Spurgeon on Prayer and Spiritual Warfare

Spurgeon on the Holy Spirit

All of Grace

C. H. SPURGEON

WHITAKER
HOUSE

Publisher's note:
The author's selection of Bible versions has been retained
whenever possible, including the Revised Version when it was
originally cited. The text of this book, however, has been edited
for the modern reader. Words, expressions, and sentence
structure have been updated for clarity and readability.

Unless otherwise indicated, Scripture quotations are from the King
James Version (KJV) of the Holy Bible. Scripture quotations marked
(RV) are taken from the Revised Version of the Holy Bible.

ALL OF GRACE

ISBN-13: 978-0-88368-857-1
ISBN-10: 0-88368-857-3
Printed in the United States of America
© 1981 by Whitaker House

Whitaker House
1030 Hunt Valley Circle
New Kensington, PA 15068
www.whitakerhouse.com

Library of Congress Cataloging-in-Publication Data
Spurgeon, C. H. (Charles Haddon), 1834--1892.
All of grace / by Charles Spurgeon.
p.   cm.
ISBN 0-88368-857-3 (pbk.)
1. Salvation.   2. Grace (Theology)   I. Title.
BT751.3 .S87 2003
234—dc21   2002013587

---

3 4 5 6 7 8 9 10 11 12 **UU** 14 13 12 11 10 09 08 07

Contents

Chapter 1
To You

*Whosoever will, let him take
the water of life freely.*
—Revelation 22:17

My intention in writing this message is that many will be led to the Lord Jesus. It is sent forth in childlike dependence on the power of God the Holy Spirit to be used in the conversion of millions, if He so pleases. No doubt many men and women will read this volume, and the Lord will bless them with grace. For this reason, the clearest language has been chosen, and many simple expressions have been used. However, if scholars should happen to glance at this book, the Holy Spirit can impress them, also. Oh, that some might read this who will become great winners of souls!

Who knows how many will find their way to peace by what they read here? A more important question for you is this: Will you be one of them?

A certain man placed a fountain along a busy road. Then he hung a cup near to it by a little chain. He was told some time afterward that a great art critic had found much fault with its design. "But," he asked, "do many thirsty people drink at it?" Then they told him that thousands of poor people, men, women, and children, quenched their thirst at this fountain. He smiled and said that he was not troubled by the critic's observation. He only hoped that on some hot summer's day the critic himself might fill the cup, be refreshed, and praise the name of the Lord.

Here is my fountain, and here is my cup. Find fault if you wish, but do drink of the water of life. I care only for this. I would rather bless the soul of the poorest street cleaner or rag-gatherer than please a prince and fail to convert him to God.

Are you serious about reading these pages? If so, we are agreed at the outset. However, my goal is nothing short of your finding Christ and heaven. Oh, that we may seek this together! I do so by dedicating this book with prayer. Will you not join me by looking up to God and asking Him to bless you while you read? Providence has put these pages before you. You have a little spare time in which to read them, and you feel willing to give them your attention. These are good signs. Who knows, maybe the time of blessing has come for you. At any rate, *"the Holy Ghost saith, To day if ye will hear his voice, harden not your hearts"* (Hebrews 3:7–8).

Chapter 2
Open the Door

Behold, I stand at the door, and knock:
if any man hear my voice, and open the door,
I will come in to him.
—Revelation 3:20

I heard a story; I think it came from the north country. A minister called on a poor woman intending to help her, for he knew that she was very poor. With his money in hand, he knocked at the door, but she did not answer. He concluded she was not at home and went his way. A little later he met her at the church and told her that he had remembered her need. "I called at your house and knocked several times. I suppose you were not at home because there was no answer." "At what hour did you call, sir?" "It was about noon." "Oh, dear," she said, "I heard you, sir, and I am so sorry I did not answer. I thought it was the man calling for the rent." Many poor people know what this means. Now, it is my desire to be heard, and therefore I want to say that I am not calling for the rent. Indeed, it is not the purpose of this book to ask anything of you. I want to tell you that salvation is all of grace, which means free, gratis, for nothing.

Often when we are anxious to win attention, our listener thinks, "Oh! Now I am going to be told what to do. It is the man calling for what is due God, and I have nothing to pay it with. I will not be at home." No, this book does not come to make a demand on you, but to bring you something. We are not going to talk about law and duty and punishment, but about love and goodness and forgiveness and mercy and eternal life. Therefore, do not act as if you were not at home. Do not turn a deaf ear or a careless heart. I am asking nothing of you in the name of God or man. It is not my intent to make any requirement at your hands. I come in God's name to bring you a free gift that will be your present and eternal joy to receive.

Open the door and let my pleadings enter. *"Come now, and let us reason together"* (Isaiah 1:18). The Lord Himself invites you to a conference concerning your immediate and endless happiness. He would not have done this if He did not mean well toward you. Do not refuse the Lord Jesus who knocks at your door, for He knocks with a hand that was nailed to the tree for such as you are. Since His only and sole objective is your good, incline your ear and come to Him. Listen diligently, and let the good Word sink into your soul. It may be that the hour has come for you to enter that new life that is the beginning of heaven. *"Faith cometh by hearing"* (Romans 10:17), and reading is a type of hearing. Faith may come to you while you are reading this book. Why not? O blessed Spirit of all grace, make it so!

Chapter 3
God Justifies the Ungodly

To him that worketh not, but believeth on him
that justifieth the ungodly, his faith is
counted for righteousness.
—Romans 4:5

This message is for you: *"To him that worketh not, but believeth on him that justifieth the ungodly, his faith is counted for righteousness."*

I call your attention to the words, *"Him that justifieth the ungodly."* They seem to me to be very wonderful words.

Are you surprised that there is such an expression as that in the Bible, *"That justifieth the ungodly"*? I have heard that men who hate the doctrines of the Cross bring the charge against God that He saves wicked men and receives to Himself the vilest of the vile. See how this Scripture accepts the charge and plainly states it! By the mouth of His servant, Paul; by the inspiration of the Holy Spirit, He takes to Himself the title of *"Him that justifieth the ungodly."* He makes those just who are unjust. He forgives those who deserve no favor. Did you think that salvation was for the good and that God's grace was for the pure and holy who are free from sin? Perhaps you think that if you were excellent, then God would reward you. Maybe you have thought that, because you are not worthy, there could be no way for you to enjoy His favor. You must be somewhat surprised to read a text like this: *"Him that justifieth the ungodly."* I do not wonder at your surprise. For, with all my familiarity with the great grace of God, I never cease to wonder at it, either.

No One Is Righteous before God

It does sound surprising, does it not, that it should be possible for a holy God to justify an unholy man? We, according to our natural reliance on good works for our salvation, are always talking about our own goodness and our own worthiness. We stubbornly believe that there must be something in us in order to win the notice of God. Now, God, who sees through all deceptions, knows that there is no goodness whatsoever in us. He says that *"there is none righteous, no, not one"* (Romans 3:10). He knows that *"all our righteousnesses are as filthy rags"* (Isaiah 64:6). Therefore, the Lord Jesus did not come into the world expecting to find goodness and righteousness, but to bestow them upon those who do not have them. He comes, not because we *are* just, but to make us so; He *"justifieth the ungodly."*

When a lawyer comes into court, if he is an honest man, he desires to plead the case of an innocent person and justify him before the court from the things of which he has been falsely accused. It should be the lawyer's objective to justify the innocent person, and he should not attempt to protect the guilty party. It is not man's right nor in his power to truly justify the guilty. This is a miracle reserved for the Lord alone. God, the infinitely just Sovereign, knows that there is not a just man on earth who does good and does not sin. Therefore, in the infinite sovereignty of His divine nature and in the splendor of His ineffable love, He undertakes the task not so much of justifying the just as of justifying the ungodly. God has devised ways and means of making the ungodly man stand justly accepted before Him. He has set up a system by which, with perfect justice, He can treat the guilty as if he had been free from offense. Yes, He can treat him as if he were wholly free from sin. He justifies the ungodly.

*"Christ Jesus came into the world to save **sinners**"* (1 Timothy 1:15, emphasis added). This truth is a very surprising thing—a thing to be marveled

at most of all by those who enjoy it. I know that it is to me, even to this day, the greatest wonder that I have ever heard of—that God would ever justify *me*. I feel myself to be a lump of unworthiness, a mass of corruption, and a heap of sin apart from His almighty love. I know and am fully assured that I am justified by *"faith which is in Christ Jesus"* (2 Timothy 3:15). I am treated as if I had been perfectly just and made an heir of God and a joint-heir with Christ. And yet by nature, I must take my place among the most sinful. Though altogether undeserving, I am treated as if I had been deserving. I am loved with as much love as if I had always been godly, whereas before I was ungodly. Who can help being astonished at this demonstration of grace? Gratitude for such favor stands dressed in robes of wonder.

Now, while this is very surprising, I want you to notice how available it makes the Gospel to you and to me. If God justifies the ungodly, then He can justify you. Is that not the very kind of person that you are? If you are unconverted at this moment, it is a very proper description of you. You have lived without God; you have been the reverse of godly. In one word, you have been and are *ungodly*. Perhaps you have not even attended a place of worship on Sundays, but have lived in disregard of God's day and house and Word. This proves that you have been ungodly. Sadder still, it may be that you have even tried to doubt God's existence and have gone to the point of saying that you did so. You have lived on this fair earth, full of the blessings of God's presence, and all the while you have shut your eyes to the clear evidences of His power and Godhead. You have lived as if there were no God. Indeed, you would have been very pleased if you could have positively demonstrated to yourself that there is no God. Possibly you have lived a great many years this way so that you are now pretty well settled in your ways. Yet God is not in any of them. If you were to be labeled ungodly, it would describe you as well as if the sea were to be labeled salt water, would it not?

Possibly you are a person of another sort. You have regularly attended to all the outward forms of religion. Yet you have had no heart in them at all but have been truly ungodly. Though meeting with the people of God, you have never met with God yourself. You have sung in the choir and yet have not praised the Lord with your heart. You have lived without any love for God in your heart or regard for His commands in your life. Well, you are just the kind of person to whom this Gospel is sent, this Gospel that says that God justifies the ungodly. It is very wonderful and is happily available for you. It just suits you, does it not? How I wish that you would accept it! If you are a sensible person, you will see the remarkable grace of God in providing for someone such as you are. You will say to yourself, "Justify the ungodly! Why, then, should I not be justified, and justified at once?"

Self-Righteousness Is a Delusion

Now, observe further that it must be so. The salvation of God is for those who do not deserve it and have no preparation for it. It is reasonable that this statement is in the Bible, for no others need justifying but those who have no justification of their own. If any of you are perfectly righteous, you desire no justifying. You feel that you are doing your duty well and almost putting heaven under an obligation to you. What do you want with a Savior or with mercy? What do you want with justification? You will be tired of this book by this time, for it will have no interest to you.

If any of you are giving yourselves such proud airs, listen to me for a little while. You will be lost as surely as you are alive. You righteous men, whose righteousness is all of your own working, are either deceivers or deceived. Scripture cannot lie, and it says plainly, *"There is none righteous, no, not one"* (Romans 3:10).

In any case, I have no Gospel to preach to the self-righteous, no, not a word. Jesus Christ Himself did *"not come to call the righteous"* (Matthew 9:13), and I am not going to do what He did not do. If I called you, you would not come. Therefore, I will not call you. Rather, I ask you to look at that righteousness of yours until you see what a delusion it is. It is not half as substantial as a cobweb. Be finished with it! Flee from it! Believe that the only people who need justification are those who are not just in themselves. They need something to be done for them to make them just before the judgment seat of God. You can depend on this: The Lord does only what is needful. Infinite wisdom never attempts what is unnecessary. Jesus never undertakes what is superfluous. To make him just who is just is no work for God. That is a labor for a fool. However, to make him just who is unjust, that is work for infinite love and mercy. To justify the ungodly is a miracle worthy of God, and it is.

Pardon Is for the Guilty

Now, look. If there is a physician anywhere in the world who has discovered sure and precious remedies, to whom is that physician sent? To those who are perfectly healthy? I think not. Send him down to a place where there are no sick people, and he feels that he is out of place. There is nothing for him to do. *"They that are whole have no need of the physician, but they that are sick"* (Mark 2:17). Is it not equally clear that the great remedies of grace and redemption are for the sick in soul? They cannot be for the whole, for they cannot be of use to such. If you feel that you are spiritually sick, the Physician has come into the world for you. If you are altogether undone by reason of your sin, you are the very person aimed at in the plan of salvation.

I say that the Lord of love had just such as you in His eye when He arranged the system of grace. Suppose a man of generous spirit were to resolve to forgive all those who were indebted to him. It is clear that this could apply only to those really in his debt. One person owes him a thousand dollars, and another owes him fifty dollars; each one has but to have his bill receipted, and the liability is wiped out. However, the most generous person cannot forgive the debts of those who do not owe him anything. It is out of the power of Omnipotence to forgive where there is no sin. Pardon, therefore, cannot be for you who have no sin. Pardon must be for the guilty. Forgiveness must be for the sinful. It would be absurd to talk of forgiving those who do not need forgiveness or pardoning those who have never offended.

Do you think that you must be lost because you are a sinner? This is the reason you can be saved. Because you realize that you are a sinner, I would encourage you to believe that grace is ordained for such as you. The hymnwriter Joseph Hart even dared to say,

> A sinner is a sacred thing;
> The Holy Ghost hath made him so.

It is true that Jesus seeks and saves those who are lost (Luke 19:10). He died and made a real atonement for real sinners. When men are not playing with words or calling themselves "miserable sinners" in false humility, I feel overjoyed to meet with them. I would be glad to talk all night to bona fide sinners. The inn of mercy never closes its doors on such, neither on weekdays nor on Sunday. Our Lord Jesus did not die for imaginary sins. His heart's blood was spilled to wash out deep crimson stains that nothing else can remove.

He who is a dirty sinner is the kind of man that Jesus Christ came to make clean. A gospel preacher on one occasion preached a sermon from the verse, *"Now also the ax is laid unto the root of the trees"* (Luke 3:9). He delivered such a sermon that one of his hearers said to him, "One would have thought that you had been preaching to criminals. Your sermon ought to have been delivered in the county jail." "Oh, no," said the good man, "if I were preaching in the county jail, I would not preach from that text. There I would preach, *'This is a faithful saying, and worthy of all acceptation, that Christ Jesus came into the world to save sinners'* (1 Timothy 1:15). This is true." The law is for the self-righteous, to humble their pride. The Gospel is for the lost, to remove their despair.

Come Just as You Are

I want to make this very plain. I hope that I have done so already. Yet, still, plain as it is, it is only the Lord who can make a man see it. At first it does seem most amazing to man that salvation would really be for him when he is lost and guilty. He thinks that it must be for him when he is penitent, forgetting that his penitence is a part of his salvation. "Oh," he says, "but I must be this and that," all of which is true, for he will be this and that as the result of salvation. However, salvation comes to him before he has any of the results of salvation. In fact, it comes to him while he deserves only this bare, beggarly, base, abominable description: *ungodly.* That is all he is when God's Gospel comes to justify him.

Therefore, may I urge any who have no good thing about them—who fear that they do not have even a good feeling or anything at all that can recommend them to God—to firmly believe that our gracious God is able and willing to take them without anything to recommend them. He is willing to forgive them spontaneously, not because *they* are good, but because *He* is good. Does He not make His sun to shine on the evil as well as on the good? Does He not give fruitful seasons and send the rain and the sunshine in their time even on the most ungodly nations? (See Matthew 5:45.) Yes, even Sodom had its sun and Gomorrah had its dew. The great grace of God surpasses my conception and your conception. I would like you to think worthily of it. As high as the heavens are above the earth, so high are God's thoughts above our thoughts (Isaiah 55:9). He can *"abundantly pardon"* (v. 7). *"Christ Jesus came into the world to save sinners"* (1 Timothy 1:15); forgiveness is for the guilty.

Do not attempt to touch yourself up and make yourself something other than what you really are. Come as you are to Him who justifies the ungodly. Some time ago, a great artist had painted a picture of a part of the city in which he lived. He wanted, for historic purposes, to include in his picture certain characters well known in the town. A street sweeper, who was unkempt, ragged, and filthy, was known to everybody, and there was a suitable place for him in the picture. The artist said to this ragged and rugged individual, "I will pay you well if you will come down to my studio and let me paint you." He came around in the morning but was soon sent away for he had washed his face, combed his hair, and donned a respectable suit of clothes. He was needed as a beggar and was not invited in any other capacity. In the same way, the Gospel will receive you into its halls if you come as a sinner, not otherwise. Do not wait for reformation, but come at once for salvation. God justifies the *ungodly,* and that takes you up where you are now. It meets you in your worst state.

Come in your disorder. I mean, come to your heavenly Father in all your sin and sinfulness. Come to Jesus just as you are: leprous, filthy, naked, neither fit to live nor fit to die. Come, you who are the very sweepings of creation. Come, though you hardly dare to hope for anything but death. Come, though despair is brooding over you, pressing on your heart like a horrible nightmare. Come and ask the Lord to justify another ungodly one. Why should He not? Come, for this great mercy of God is meant for such as you. I put it in the language of the text, and I cannot put it more strongly: The Lord God Himself takes to Himself this gracious title, *"Him that justifieth the ungodly."* He makes just, and causes to be treated as just, those who by nature are ungodly. Is that not a wonderful word for you? Do not delay in considering this matter well.

Chapter 4
"It Is God That Justifieth"

It is God that justifieth.
—Romans 8:33

I t is a wonderful thing to be justified, or made just. If we had never broken the laws of God, we would not have needed justification, for we would have been just in ourselves. He who has always done the things that he should have done, and has never done anything that he should not have done, is justified by the law. However, I am quite sure that you are not one of that sort. You are too honest to pretend to be without sin, and therefore you need to be justified.

Now, if you justify yourself, you will simply be a self-deceiver. Therefore, do not attempt it. It is never worthwhile. If you ask your fellowmen to justify you, what can they do? You can make some of them speak well of you, for small favors; and others will backbite you for less. Their judgment is not worth much.

Our text says, *"It is God that justifieth."* This is much more to the point. It is an astonishing fact, and one that we should consider with care. Come and see.

A Plan Only God Could Think Of

In the first place, nobody else but God ever would have thought of justifying those who are guilty. They have lived in open rebellion. They have done evil with both hands and have gone from bad to worse. They have turned back to sin even after they have smarted for it and have, therefore, been forced to leave it for a while. They have broken the law of God and trampled on the Gospel. They have refused proclamations of mercy and have persisted in ungodliness. How can they be forgiven and justified? Their fellowmen, despairing of them, say, "They are hopeless cases." Even Christians look on them with sorrow rather than with hope. But not so their God. He, in the splendor of His electing grace, having chosen them *"before the foundation of the world"* (Ephesians 1:4), will not rest until He has justified them and made them to be *"accepted in the beloved"* (v. 6). Is it not written, *"Whom he did predestinate, them he also called: and whom he called, them he also justified: and whom he justified, them he also glorified"* (Romans 8:30)? Thus you see there are some whom the Lord resolves to justify. Why should you and I not be among them?

No one but God ever would have thought of justifying me. I am a wonder to myself. I do not doubt that grace is equally viewed as such by others. Look at Saul of Tarsus, who foamed at the mouth against God's servants. Like a hungry wolf, he worried the lambs and the sheep right and left. And yet God struck him down on the road to Damascus and changed his heart. (See Acts 8:3; 9:1–22.) God so fully justified him that, before long, this man became the greatest preacher of justification by faith who ever lived. He often must have marveled that he was justified by faith in Christ Jesus, for he was once a determined stickler for salvation by the works of the law. None but God ever would have thought of justifying such a man as Saul the persecutor. Yet the Lord God is glorious in grace.

A Plan Only God Could Fulfill

Even if anybody *had* thought of justifying the ungodly, no one but God could have done it. It is quite impossible for any person to forgive offenses that have not been committed against himself. A person has greatly injured you. You can forgive him, and I hope you will, but no third person can forgive him apart from you. If the wrong is done to you, the pardon must come from you. If we have sinned against God, it is in God's power to forgive, for the sin is against Himself. That is why David said in Psalm 51:4, *"Against thee, thee only, have I sinned, and done this evil in thy sight,"* for then God, against whom the offense was committed, could put the offense away.

What we owe to God, our great Creator can remit if it so pleases Him. And, if He remits it, it is remitted. No one but the great God against whom we have committed the sin can blot out that sin. Therefore, let us see that we go to Him and seek mercy at His hands. Do not let us be led aside by those who would have us confess to them; they have no warrant in the Word of God for their pretensions. Yet even if they were ordained to pronounce absolution in God's name, it would still be better for us to go to the great Lord through Jesus Christ, the Mediator, and seek and find pardon at His hands, since we are sure that this is the right way. Proxy Christianity involves too great a risk. You had better see to your soul's matters yourself and leave them in no man's hands.

Only God can justify the ungodly, but He can do it to perfection. He casts our sins behind His back (Isaiah 38:17); He blots them out (Isaiah 43:25). He says that, although they are sought after, they will not be found (Jeremiah 50:20).

With no other reason for it but His own infinite goodness, He has prepared a glorious way by which He can make scarlet sins *"as white as snow"* (Isaiah 1:18). He can remove our transgressions from us *"as far as the east is from the west"* (Psalm 103:12). He says, *"Their sins and iniquities will I remember no more"* (Hebrews 10:17). He goes the length of making an end of sin. One of old called out in amazement, *"Who is a God like unto thee, that pardoneth iniquity, and passeth by the transgression of the remnant of his heritage? he retaineth not his anger for ever, because he delighteth in mercy"* (Micah 7:18).

We are not now speaking of justice, nor of God's dealing with men according to what they deserve. If you profess to deal with the righteous Lord on legal grounds, everlasting wrath threatens you, for that is what you deserve. Blessed be His name, *"He hath not dealt with us after* [according to] *our sins"* (Psalm 103:10), but now He deals with us in terms of free grace and infinite compassion, and He says, "I will receive you graciously and love you freely." (See Hosea 14:2, 4.) Believe it, for it is certainly true that the great God is able to treat the guilty with abundant mercy. Yes, He is able to treat the ungodly as if they had always been godly.

Read carefully the parable of the prodigal son, and see how the forgiving father received the returning wanderer with as much love as if he

had never gone away and had never defiled himself with prostitutes. He carried this so far that
the elder brother began to grumble at it, but
the father never withdrew his love. (See Luke
15:11–32.) However guilty you may be, if you will
only come back to your God and Father, He will
treat you as if you had never done wrong! He will
regard you as just, and deal with you accordingly.
What do you say to this?

Do you not see—for I want to clearly bring
out what a splendid thing it is—that, as no one
but God would think of justifying the ungodly,
and no one but God could do it, yet the Lord can
do it? See how the apostle puts the challenge:
*"Who shall lay any thing to the charge of God's
elect? It is God that justifieth"* (Romans 8:33).
If God has justified a man, it is well done; it is
rightly done; it is justly done; it is everlastingly
done.

The Highest Court Can Pronounce You Just

I read a statement in a magazine that is full of
venom against the Gospel and those who preach
it. It said that we hold some kind of theory by
which we imagine that sin can be removed from
men. We hold no theory; we publish a fact. The
grandest fact under heaven is this: Christ, by His
precious blood, does actually put away sin. And
God, for Christ's sake dealing with men on terms

of divine mercy, forgives the guilty and justifies them—not according to anything that He sees in them or foresees will be in them, but according to the riches of His mercy, which lie in His own heart. This we have preached, do preach, and will preach as long as we live. *"It is God that justifieth"* the ungodly. He is not ashamed of doing it, nor are we of preaching it.

The justification that comes from God Himself must be beyond question. If the Judge acquits me, who can condemn me? If the highest court in the universe has pronounced me just, who will lay anything to my charge? Justification from God is a sufficient answer to an awakened conscience. The Holy Spirit, by His means, breathes peace over our entire nature, and we are no longer afraid. With this justification, we can answer all the roarings and railings of Satan and ungodly men. With this we will be able to die. With this we will boldly rise again and face the last great court of justice.

> Bold shall I stand in that great day,
>   For who aught to my charge shall lay?
> While by my Lord absolved I am,
>   From sin's tremendous curse and
>   blame.   —Count Zinzendorf

The Lord can blot out all your sins. I make no shot in the dark when I say this. *"All manner of sin and blasphemy shall be forgiven unto men"*

(Matthew 12:31). Though you are steeped up to your throat in crime, He can, with a word, remove the defilement and say, *"I will; be thou clean"* (Mark 1:41). The Lord is a great forgiver.

I believe in the forgiveness of sins. Do you?

He can even at this hour pronounce the sentence, "Your sins are forgiven; go in peace." If He does this, no power in heaven or earth or under the earth can put you under suspicion, much less under wrath. Do not doubt the power of almighty love. You could not forgive your fellowman if he offended you as you have offended God. However, you must not measure God's corn with your bushel. His thoughts and ways are as much above yours as the heavens are high above the earth (Isaiah 55:9).

"Well," you say, "it would be a great miracle if the Lord were to pardon me." Indeed, it would be a supreme miracle. Therefore, He is likely to do it, for He does *"great things and unsearchable"* (Job 5:9) that we did not look for.

Look to Jesus

I myself was stricken with a horrible sense of guilt that made my life a misery. Yet when I heard the command, *"Look unto me, and be ye saved, all the ends of the earth: for I am God, and there is none else"* (Isaiah 45:22), I looked, and in a moment the Lord justified me. Jesus Christ, crucified for me, was what I saw, and that sight gave me rest. When those who were bitten by the fiery serpents in the wilderness looked to the serpent of brass, they were healed at once. (See Numbers 21:5–9.) Likewise, I was healed when I looked to the crucified Savior. The Holy Spirit, who enabled me to believe, gave me peace through believing. I felt as sure that I was forgiven as I had felt sure of condemnation before. I had been certain of my condemnation because the Word of God declared it and my conscience bore witness to it. However, when the Lord justified me, I was made equally certain by the same witnesses. The word of the Lord in the Scripture says, *"He that believeth on him is not condemned"* (John 3:18). My conscience bears witness that I believed and that, in pardoning me, God is just. Thus I have the witness of the Holy Spirit and my own conscience, and these two agree. Oh, how I wish you would receive the testimony of God on this matter, for then you also would soon have the witness in yourself!

I venture to say that a sinner justified by God stands on a surer footing than even a righteous man justified by his works, if there is such. Yet, if we were in that situation, we could never be sure that we had done enough works. Our consciences would always be uneasy for fear that, after all, we would fall short and have only the trembling verdict of a fallible judgment to rely on. However, when God Himself justifies, and the Holy Spirit bears witness to this fact by giving us peace with God, then we feel that the matter is sure and settled, and we enter into rest. No tongue can tell the depth of the calm that comes over the soul that has received the *"peace of God, which passeth all understanding"* (Philippians 4:7).

Chapter 5

"Just, and the Justifier"

That he might be just, and the justifier of him which believeth in Jesus.
—Romans 3:26

We have seen that the ungodly can be justified, and we have considered the great truth that only God can justify any man. We now come a step further and make the inquiry, How can a just God justify guilty men? We find a full answer in the words of Paul in Romans 3:21–26. We will read these six verses in order to get the main idea of the passage:

> But now the righteousness of God without the law is manifested, being witnessed by the law and the prophets; even the righteousness of God which is by faith of

Jesus Christ unto all and upon all them that believe: for there is no difference: for all have sinned, and come short of the glory of God; being justified freely by his grace through the redemption that is in Christ Jesus: whom God hath set forth to be a propitiation through faith in his blood, to declare his righteousness for the remission of sins that are past, through the forbearance of God; to declare, I say, at this time his righteousness: that he might be just, and the justifier of him which believeth in Jesus.

Let me give you a bit of personal experience. When I was under the conviction of sin, under the hand of the Holy Spirit, I had a clear and sharp sense of the justice of God. Sin, whatever it might be to other people, became to me an intolerable burden. It was not so much that I feared hell, but that I feared sin. I knew myself to be so horribly guilty that I remember feeling that if God did not punish me for sin, He should do so. I felt that the Judge of all the earth ought to condemn such sin as mine. I sat on the judgment seat and condemned myself to perish, for I confessed that if I had been God, I could have done nothing else than send such a guilty person as I was down to the lowest hell.

All the while, I had on my mind a deep concern for the honor of God's name and the integrity of

His moral government. I felt that my conscience would not be satisfied if I could be unjustly forgiven. The sin I had committed must be punished. However, then there was the question of how God could be just and yet justify me who had been so guilty. I asked my heart, "How can He be just and yet be the Justifier?" I was worried and wearied with this question; I could see no answer to it. Certainly, I could never have invented an answer that would have satisfied my conscience.

Christ Is Our Representative and Our Covenant Head

The doctrine of the Atonement is, to my mind, one of the surest proofs of the divine inspiration of Holy Scripture. Who would or could have thought of the just Christ dying for the unjust rebel? This is no teaching of human mythology or dream of poetic imagination. This method of atonement is known among men only because it is a fact. Fiction could not have devised it. God Himself ordained it; it is not a matter that could have been imagined.

I had heard the plan of salvation by the sacrifice of Jesus from my youth, but I did not know any more about it in my innermost soul than if I had been born and bred a heathen. The light was there, but I was blind. It was necessary for the Lord Himself to make it plain to me. It came to me as a new revelation, as fresh as if I had never read in Scripture that Jesus was declared to be the propitiation for sins so that God might be just (Romans 3:25). I believe that the glorious doctrine of the substitution of the Lord Jesus will have to come as a revelation to every newborn child of God when he sees it. I came to understand that salvation is possible through vicarious sacrifice, and that provision had been made in the first constitution and arrangement of things for such a substitution.

I was made to see that He who is the Son of God, coequal and coeternal with the Father, had of old been made the covenant Head of a chosen people so that He might in that capacity suffer for them and save them. Inasmuch as our fall was not at first a personal one, for we fell by the first Adam, it became possible for us to be recovered by a second Representative. We are saved by Him who has undertaken to be the covenant Head of His people in order to be their Second Adam. I saw that before I had actually sinned, I had fallen by my first father's sin. I rejoiced that therefore it became possible in point of law for me to rise by a second Head and Representative. The fall by Adam left a loophole of escape; another Adam could undo the ruin made by the first.

When I was anxious about the possibility of a just God pardoning me, I understood and saw by faith that He who is the Son of God became man. In His own blessed person He bore my sin *"in his own body on the tree"* (1 Peter 2:24). I saw that the chastisement of my peace was laid on Him, and that with His stripes I was healed (Isaiah 53:5). Have you ever seen that? Have you ever understood how God can be just to the fullest extent, not remitting penalty nor blunting the edge of the sword, and yet can be infinitely merciful and can justify the ungodly who turn to Him?

It is because the Son of God, supremely glorious in His matchless person, undertook the vindication of the law by bearing the sentence due to me that God is therefore able to pass by my sin. The law of God was more vindicated by the death of Christ than it would have been had all transgressors been sent to hell. For the Son of God to suffer for sin was a more glorious establishment of the government of God than for the whole race to suffer.

Jesus has borne the death penalty on our behalf. Behold the wonder! There He hangs on the cross! This is the greatest sight you will ever see. There He hangs, Son of God and Son of Man, bearing pains unutterable, the Just for the unjust, to bring us to God. Oh, the glory of that sight! The Innocent punished! The Holy One condemned! The ever blessed One made a curse! The infinitely glorious One put to a shameful death! The more I look at the sufferings of the Son of God, the more I am sure that they must meet my case. Why did He suffer if not to take the penalty away from us?

If, then, He took it away by His death, it is surely taken. Those who believe in Him need not fear it. It must be that, since atonement is made, God is able to forgive without disrupting the basis of His throne or in the least degree blotting the statute book. Conscience gets a full answer to her tremendous question.

The wrath of God against iniquity must be terrible beyond all conception. Moses said it well: *"Who knoweth the power of thine anger?"* (Psalm 90:11). Yet when we hear the Lord of glory cry, *"Why hast thou forsaken me?"* (Matthew 27:46), and see Him yielding up His spirit (v. 50), we feel that the justice of God has been abundantly vindicated by the divine Jesus' perfect obedience and terrible death. If God Himself bows before His own law, what more can be done? There is more in the Atonement by way of merit than there is in all human sin by way of demerit.

The great gulf of Jesus' loving self-sacrifice can swallow up the mountains of our sins—all of them. For the sake of the infinite good of this one representative Man, the Lord may well look with favor on other men. He does so, however unworthy they may be in and of themselves. It was a miracle of miracles that the Lord Jesus Christ would stand in our stead and

> Bear that we might never bear
> His Father's righteous ire.

"Just, and the Justifier"

Yet He has done so. *"It is finished"* (John 19:30). God will spare the sinner because He did not spare His Son. God can pass by your transgressions because He laid them upon His only begotten Son nearly two thousand years ago. If you believe in Jesus (that is the point), then your sins were carried away by Him who was the Scapegoat for His people.

Trust Him Wholly and Entirely

What is it to believe in Him? It is not merely to say, "He is God and the Savior," but to trust Him wholly and entirely and take Him for all your salvation from this time forth and forever as your Lord, your Master, your all. If you will have Jesus, He has you already. If you believe in Him, I tell you that you cannot go to hell, for then Christ's death would be in vain. A sacrifice cannot be made and then withheld from the one for whom it was given. If the believing soul could be condemned, then why a sacrifice? If Jesus died in my stead, why should I die, also?

Every believer can claim that the sacrifice was actually made for him. By faith he has laid his hands on it and made it his own, and therefore he may rest assured that he can never perish. The Lord would not receive this offering on our behalf and then condemn us to die. The Lord cannot read our pardon written in the blood of His own Son and then smite us. That would be impossible. Oh, that you may at once have grace given to you to look to Jesus and to begin at the beginning—with Jesus, the Fountainhead of mercy to guilty man!

He *"justifieth the ungodly"* (Romans 4:5). *"It is God that justifieth"* (Romans 8:33). Therefore, and for that reason only, it can be done. He does it through the atoning sacrifice of His divine Son. Therefore, it can be justly done—so justly done that no one will ever question it. It can be so thoroughly done that, in the last tremendous Day, when heaven and earth will pass away, there will be none who deny the validity of the justification. *"Who is he that condemneth? It is Christ that died....Who shall lay any thing to the charge of God's elect? It is God that justifieth"* (Romans 8:34, 33).

Now will you come into this lifeboat just as you are? Here is safety from the wreck! Accept the sure deliverance. "I have nothing with me," you say. You are not asked to bring anything with you. Men who escape for their lives will leave even their clothes behind. Leap for it just as you are.

I will tell you something about myself to encourage you. My sole hope for heaven lies in the full atonement made on Calvary's cross for the ungodly. I firmly rely on that. I do not have a shadow of hope anywhere else. You are in the same condition as I am. Neither of us has anything of our own worth to be a basis of trust. Let us join hands and stand together at the foot of the cross and trust our souls once and for all to Him who shed His blood for the guilty. We will be saved by one and the same Savior. If you perish trusting Him, I must perish, too. What can I do to further prove my own confidence in the Gospel that I set before you?

Chapter 6

Deliverance from Sinning

A new heart also will I give you,
and a new spirit will I put within you.
—Ezekiel 36:26

I would like to say a word or two to those who understand the method of justification by faith that is in Christ Jesus, but who have a hard time refraining from sin. We can never be happy, restful, or spiritually healthy until we become holy. We must get rid of sin. Yet how can we? This is the life-or-death question of many. The old nature is very strong, and they have tried to curb and tame it. However, it will not be subdued. They find themselves, though anxious to be better, if anything, growing worse than before.

The heart is so hard, the will is so obstinate, the passions are so furious, the thoughts are so volatile, the imagination is so ungovernable, the desires are so wild, that man feels as if he has a den of wild beasts within him. He feels that they will devour him sooner than they will be ruled by him. We may say of our fallen nature what the Lord said to Job concerning Leviathan: *"Wilt thou play with him as with a bird? or wilt thou bind him for thy maidens?"* (Job 41:5). A man might as well hope to hold the north wind in the palm of his hand as expect to control, by his own strength, those boisterous powers that exist within his fallen nature. This is a greater feat than any of the fabled labors of Hercules; God is needed here.

"I could believe that Jesus would forgive sin," says one, "but my trouble is that I sin again and that I feel such awful tendencies to evil within me. As surely as a stone flung into the air soon comes down again to the ground, so do I, though I am sent up to heaven by earnest preaching, return again to my insensible state. I am easily fascinated with the spellbinding eyes of sin. I am thus held, as if under a spell, so that I cannot escape from my own folly."

Salvation would be a sadly incomplete promise if it did not deal with this part of our ruined state. We need to be purified as well as pardoned. Justification without sanctification would not be salvation at all. It would call the leper clean and leave him to die of his disease. It would forgive the rebellion and allow the rebel to remain an enemy to his king. It would remove the consequences but overlook the cause, and this would leave an endless and hopeless task before us. It would stop the stream for a time but leave an open fountain of defilement that would sooner or later break forth with increased power. Remember that the Lord Jesus came to take away sin in three ways. He came to remove the penalty of sin, the power of sin, and last, the presence of sin. At once you may reach the second part—the power of sin may immediately be broken—and so you will be on the road to the third—the removal of the presence of sin. We *"know that he was manifested to take away our sins"* (1 John 3:5).

The angel said of our Lord, *"Thou shalt call his name Jesus: for he shall save his people from their sins"* (Matthew 1:21). Our Lord Jesus came to destroy in us the works of the devil. What was said at our Lord's birth was also declared in His death. When the soldier pierced His side, blood and water came out to set forth the double cleansing by which we are delivered from the guilt and the defilement of sin.

If, however, you are troubled about the power of sin and about the tendencies of your nature, as you may well be, here is a promise for you. Have faith in it, for it stands in that covenant of grace that is ordered and sure in all things. God, who cannot lie, has said in Ezekiel 36:26, *"A new heart also will I give you, and a new spirit will I put within you: and I will take away the stony heart out of your flesh, and I will give you an heart of flesh."*

You see, it is all *"I will"* and *"I will." "I will give"* and *"I will take away."* This is the royal style of the King of Kings, who is able to accomplish all His will. No word of His will ever fall to the ground.

God's Power Defeats Sin

The Lord knows very well that you cannot change your own heart and cannot cleanse your own nature. However, He also knows that He can do both. He can cause the Ethiopian to change his skin and the leopard his spots. (See Jeremiah 13:23.) Hear this and be astonished: He can create you a second time; He can cause you to be born again. This is a miracle of grace, but the Holy Spirit will perform it. It would be very wonderful if one could stand at the foot of Niagara Falls and speak a word that would make the Niagara River begin to run upstream and leap up that great precipice over which it now rolls down with stupendous force. Nothing but the power of God could achieve that marvel. Yet that would be more than a fit parallel to what would take place if the course of your nature were altogether reversed.

Deliverance from Sinning

All things are possible with God (Matthew 19:26). He can reverse the direction of your desires and the current of your life. Instead of going downward from God, He can make your whole being tend upward toward God. In fact, that is what the Lord has promised to do for all who are in the covenant, and we know from Scripture that all believers are in the covenant. Let me read the words again: *"A new spirit will I put within you: and I will take away the stony heart out of your flesh, and I will give you an heart of flesh"* (Ezekiel 36:26).

What a wonderful promise! And it is *"yea"* and *"Amen"* in Christ Jesus to the glory of God (2 Corinthians 1:20). Let us lay hold of it, accept it as true, and appropriate it to ourselves. Then it will be fulfilled in us, and we will, after days and years, sing of that wondrous change that the sovereign grace of God has made in us.

God Will Transform You

It is worth considering that, when the Lord takes away the stony heart, the deed is done. Once that is done, no known power can ever take away the new heart that He gives and the right spirit that He puts within us. "The gifts and calling of God are without repentance" (Romans 11:29), that is, without repentance on His part. He does not take away what He once has given. Let Him renew you, and you will be renewed. Man's reformations

49

and cleansings soon come to an end, for the dog returns to his vomit (Proverbs 26:11). However, when God puts a new heart in us, the new heart is there forever, and it will never harden into stone again. He who made it flesh will keep it so. Herein we may rejoice and be forever glad of what God creates in the king-dom of His grace.

To put the matter very simply, did you ever hear of Rowland Hill's illustration of the cat and the sow? I will give it in my own fashion to illustrate our Savior's expressive words, *"Ye must be born again"* (John 3:7). Do you see that cat? What a clean animal she is! How cleverly she washes herself with her tongue and her paws! It is quite a pretty sight! Did you ever see a sow do that? No, you never did. It is contrary to its nature. It prefers to wallow in the mud. Go and teach a sow to wash itself, and see how little success you will have. It would be a great sanitary improvement if swine would be clean. Teach them to wash and clean them-selves as the cat has been doing! It is a useless task. You may by force wash that sow, but it quickly runs to the mud and is soon as foul as ever. The only way in which you can get a sow to wash itself is to transform it into a cat. But not until then will it wash itself and be clean.

Suppose that transformation had been accomplished. Then what was difficult or impossible is easy enough—the swine will henceforth be fit for your parlor and your hearth rug. So it is with an ungodly man; you cannot force him to do what a renewed man does most willingly. You may teach him and set him a good example, but he cannot learn the art of holiness because he does not want to. His nature leads him another way. When the Lord makes a new man of him, then all things bear a different mark. So great is this change that I once heard a convert say, "Either all the world is changed, or else I am." The new nature follows after right as naturally as the old nature wanders after wrong. What a blessing to receive such a nature! Only the Holy Spirit can give it.

Did it ever strike you how wonderful it is for the Lord to give a new heart and a right spirit to a man? Perhaps you have seen a lobster that has fought with another lobster and lost one of its claws, and a new claw has grown. That is a remarkable thing. However, it is much more astounding that a man should have a new heart given to him. This, indeed, is a miracle beyond the powers of nature. Imagine a tree. If you cut off one of its limbs, another one may grow in its place. Yet can you change the tree? Can you sweeten sour sap? Can you make the thorn bear figs? You can graft something better into it—that is the analogy that nature gives us of the work of grace—but to absolutely change the vital sap of the tree would be a miracle, indeed. God works such a mystery of power in all who believe in Jesus.

All of Grace

If you yield yourself up to His divine working, the Lord will alter your nature. He will subdue the old nature and breathe new life into you. Put your trust in the Lord Jesus Christ. He will take the stony heart out of your flesh and give you a heart of flesh. Where everything was hard, everything will be tender; where everything was depraved, everything will be virtuous; where everything tended downward, everything will rise upward with impetuous force. The lion of anger will give place to the lamb of meekness. The raven of uncleanness will fly before the dove of purity. The vile serpent of deceit will be trodden under the heel of truth.

I have seen with my own eyes such marvelous changes of moral and spiritual character that I despair of no one. I could, if it were fitting, point out those who were once unchaste women who are now pure, and blaspheming men who now delight everyone around them by their intense devotion. Thieves are made honest, drunkards sober, liars truthful, and scoffers zealous for God. Wherever the grace of God has appeared to a man, it has trained him to deny *"ungodliness and worldly lusts,"* and to *"live soberly, righteously, and godly, in this present world"* (Titus 2:12). It will do the same for you.

"I cannot make this change," says someone. Who said you could? The Scripture that we have quoted does not speak of what man will do, but of what God will do. It is God's promise, and it is for Him to fulfill His own commitments. Trust in Him to fulfill His Word to you, and it will be done.

"But how is it to be done?" What business is that of yours? Must the Lord explain His methods before you will believe Him? The Lord's working in this matter is a great mystery; the Holy Spirit performs it. He who made the promise has the responsibility of keeping the promise; and He is equal to the occasion. God, who promises this marvelous change, will assuredly carry it out in all who receive Jesus. To all of them He gives *"power to become the sons of God"* (John 1:12).

Oh, that you would believe it! Oh, that you would do the gracious Lord the justice to believe that He can and will do this for you, great miracle though it will be! Oh, that you would believe that God cannot lie! Oh, that you would trust Him for a new heart and a right spirit, for He can give them to you! May the Lord give you faith in His promise, faith in His Son, faith in the Holy Spirit, and faith in Him. To Him will be praise and honor and glory forever and ever! Amen.

Chapter 7

By Grace through Faith

*By grace are ye saved through faith;
and that not of yourselves: it is the gift of God.*
—Ephesians 2:8

I ask you now to take a moment to adoringly observe the fountainhead of our salvation—the grace of God. *"By grace are ye saved."* God is gracious; therefore, sinful men are forgiven, converted, purified, and saved. It is not because of anything in them or that can ever be in them that they are saved. It is because of the boundless love, goodness, pity, compassion, mercy, and grace of God. Wait a moment, then, at the wellhead. Behold the pure river of life-giving water as it proceeds *"out of the throne of God and of the Lamb"* (Revelation 22:1)!

All of Grace

How immeasurable is the grace of God! Who can calculate its breadth? Who can fathom its depth? Like all the rest of the divine attributes, it is infinite. God is full of love, for *"God is love"* (1 John 4:8). God is full of goodness; the very name *God* is short for "good." Unbounded goodness and love enter into the very essence of the Godhead. It is because His *"mercy endureth for ever"* (Psalm 107:1) that men are not destroyed; because His *"compassions fail not"* (Lamentations 3:22), sinners are brought to Him and forgiven.

Remember this or you may fall into error by fixing your minds so much on the faith that is the channel of salvation that you will forget the grace that is the fountain and source of faith itself. Faith is the work of God's grace in us. *"No man can say that Jesus is the Lord, but by the Holy Ghost"* (1 Corinthians 12:3). *"No man can come to me,"* said Jesus, *"except the Father which hath sent me draw him"* (John 6:44). So that faith, which is coming to Christ, is the result of divine drawing. Grace is the first and last moving cause of salvation. Faith, essential as it is, is only an important part of the machinery that grace employs. We are saved *"through faith,"* but salvation is *"by grace."* Sound forth those words as with the archangel's trumpet: *"By grace are ye saved."* What glad tidings for the undeserving!

Faith occupies the position of a channel or conduit pipe. Grace is the fountain and the stream.

By Grace through Faith

Faith is the aqueduct along which the flood of mercy flows down to refresh the thirsty sons of men. It is a great pity when the aqueduct is broken. It is a sad sight to see the many noble aqueducts around Rome that no longer carry water into the city. They are no longer used because the arches are broken and the marvelous structures are in ruins. The aqueduct must be kept intact to carry the current. Similarly, faith must be true and sound. It must lead right up to God and come right down to ourselves so that it may become a serviceable channel of mercy to our souls.

Still, I remind you again that faith is only the channel or aqueduct, and not the fountainhead. We must not look to it so much that we exalt it above the divine source of all blessing, which lies in the grace of God. Never make a Christ out of your faith, nor think of faith as if it were the independent source of your salvation. Our life is found in *"looking unto Jesus"* (Hebrews 12:2), not in looking to our own faith. By faith all things become possible to us. Yet the power is not in the faith but in the God in whom faith relies. Grace is the powerful engine, and faith is the chain that attaches the carriage of the soul to the great motive power. The righteousness of faith is not the moral excellence of faith but the righteousness of Jesus Christ, which faith grasps and takes as its own. The peace within the soul is not derived from contemplation of our own faith. It comes to us from Him who is our peace. Faith touches the hem of His garment, and virtue comes out of Him into the soul.

See, then, that the weakness of your faith will not destroy you. A trembling hand may receive a golden gift. The Lord's salvation can come to us even though we have faith only as a grain of mustard seed. The power lies in the grace of God and not in our faith. Great messages can be sent along slender wires. The peace-giving witness of the Holy Spirit can reach the heart by means of a threadlike faith that seems almost unable to sustain its own weight. Think more of Him to whom you look than of the look itself. You must look away even from your own looking and see nothing but Jesus and the grace of God revealed in Him.

Chapter 8
What Is Faith?

By grace are ye saved through faith;
and that not of yourselves: it is the gift of God.
—Ephesians 2:8

W hat is this faith concerning which it is said, *"By grace are ye saved through faith"*? There are many descriptions of faith, but almost all the definitions I have heard have made me understand it less than I did before I heard them. Someone said that after he read the chapter, he would "confound" it. It is very likely that he did so, though he meant to *expound* it. We may explain faith until nobody understands it. I hope I will not be guilty of that fault. Faith is the simplest of all things; perhaps it is the more difficult to explain because of its simplicity.

Three Aspects of Faith

Faith is made up of three things: knowledge, belief, and trust. Knowledge comes first.

Knowledge

"How shall they believe in him of whom they have not heard?" (Romans 10:14). I need to be informed of a fact before I can possibly believe it. *"Faith cometh by hearing"* (v. 17). We must first hear so that we may know what is to be believed. *"They that know thy name will put their trust in thee"* (Psalm 9:10). A measure of knowledge is essential to faith; hence the importance of acquiring knowledge. *"Incline your ear, and come unto me: hear, and your soul shall live"* (Isaiah 55:3). Such was the word of the ancient prophet, and it is still the word of the Gospel. Search the Scriptures and learn what the Holy Spirit teaches concerning Christ and His salvation. Seek to know God, *"for he that cometh to God must believe that he is, and that he is a rewarder of them that diligently seek him"* (Hebrews 11:6). May the Holy Spirit give you *"the spirit of knowledge and of the fear of the LORD"* (Isaiah 11:2)!

Know the Gospel. Know what the Good News is and how it talks of free forgiveness, change of heart, adoption into the family of God, and countless other blessings. Especially know Christ Jesus the Son of God, the Savior of men, united to us by His human nature and yet one with God. Thus He was able to act as Mediator between God and man. He was able to lay His hand on both and be the connecting link between the sinner and the Judge of all the earth. Endeavor to know more and more of Christ Jesus. Endeavor especially to know the doctrine of the sacrifice of Christ, for the main point that addresses saving faith itself is this: *"God was in Christ, reconciling the world unto himself, not imputing their trespasses unto them"* (2 Corinthians 5:19). Know that Jesus was *"made a curse for us: for it is written, Cursed is every one that hangeth on a tree"* (Galatians 3:13). Drink deep of the doctrine of the substitutionary work of Christ, for therein lies the sweetest possible comfort to the guilty sons of men, since the Lord *"made him to be sin for us...that we might be made the righteousness of God in him"* (2 Corinthians 5:21). Faith begins with knowledge.

Belief

The mind goes on to believe that these things are true. The soul believes that God is and that He hears the cries of sincere hearts. The soul believes that the Gospel is from God and that justification by faith is the grand truth that God has revealed in these last days by His Spirit more clearly than before. Then the heart believes that Jesus is verily and in truth our God and Savior, the Redeemer of men, the Prophet, Priest, and King of His people. All this is accepted as sure truth, not to be questioned. I pray that you may at once come to this. Firmly believe that *"the blood of Jesus Christ his* [God's] *Son cleanseth us from all sin"* (1 John 1:7). Believe that His sacrifice is complete and fully accepted by God on man's behalf, so that he who believes in Jesus is not condemned (John 3:17–18). Believe these truths as you believe any other statements, for the difference between ordinary faith and saving faith lies mainly in the subjects in which it is placed. Believe the witness of God just as you believe the testimony of your own father or friend. *"If we receive the witness of men, the witness of God is greater"* (1 John 5:9).

Trust

So far, you have made an advance toward faith; only one more ingredient is needed to complete it—trust. Commit yourself to the merciful God; rest your hope on the gracious Gospel. Trust your soul to the dying and living Savior; wash away your sins in the atoning blood; accept His perfect righteousness, and all will be well. Trust is the lifeblood of faith; there is no saving faith without it. The Puritans were accustomed to explaining faith by the word *recumbency*. It meant leaning upon a thing. Lean with all your weight upon Christ. An even better illustration is this: Fall at full length and lie upon the Rock of Ages. Cast yourself upon Jesus. Rest in Him. Commit yourself to Him. That done, you have exercised saving faith. Faith is not a blind thing, for faith begins with knowledge. It is not a speculative thing, for faith believes facts of which it is sure. It is not an impractical, dreamy thing, for faith trusts and

stakes its destiny on the truth of revelation. That
is one way of describing what faith is.

Faith Believes in the Person of Christ

Let me try again. Faith is believing that Christ
is what He is said to be and that He will do what
He has promised to do. Faith expects this of Him.
The Scriptures speak of Jesus Christ as being
God in human flesh, as being perfect in His character, as being made a sin offering on our behalf,
and as bearing *"our sins in his own body on the
tree"* (1 Peter 2:24). The Scripture speaks of Him
as having finished transgression, made an end
of sin, and brought in everlasting righteousness
(Daniel 9:24).

The sacred records further tell us that He *"rose
again"* (1 Corinthians 15:4) from the dead, and
that He *"ever liveth to make intercession for* [us]"
(Hebrews 7:25). The Scriptures also say that He
has gone up into glory and has taken possession
of heaven on behalf of His people. He will shortly
come again *"to judge the earth: with righteousness, shall he judge the world, and the people
with equity"* (Psalm 98:9). We are to believe most
firmly that it is so, for this was the testimony of
God the Father when He said, *"This is my beloved
Son: hear him"* (Luke 9:35). This also is testified
by God the Holy Spirit, for the Spirit has borne
witness to Christ—in the inspired Word, by many

miracles, and by His working in the hearts of men. We are to believe this testimony to be true.

Faith also believes that Christ will do what He has promised. Since He has promised to cast out none who come to Him (John 6:37), it is certain that He will not cast us out if we come to Him. Faith believes that since Jesus said, *"The water that I shall give him shall be in him a well of water springing up into everlasting life"* (John 4:14), it must be true. Faith believes that if we get this living water from Christ, it will abide in us and will well up within us in streams of holy life. Whatever Christ has promised to do, He will do, and we must believe this in order to look for pardon, justification, preservation, and eternal glory from His hands, since He has promised them to believers in Him.

Then comes the next necessary step. Jesus is what He is said to be. Jesus will do what He says He will do. Therefore, we must each trust Him, saying, "He will be to me what He says He is, and He will do to me what He has promised to do. I leave myself in the hands of Him who is appointed to save, so that He may save me. I rest on His promise that He will do even as He has said." This is saving faith, and he who has it has everlasting life. Whatever his dangers and difficulties, whatever his darkness and depression, whatever his infirmities and sins, he who believes thus on Christ Jesus is not condemned and will never come into condemnation.

What Is Faith?

May that explanation be of some service! I trust it may be used by the Spirit of God to direct you into immediate peace. *"Be not afraid, only believe"* (Mark 5:36). Trust, and be at rest.

Do Not Delay

My fear is that you will rest content with understanding what is to be done and yet never do it. The poorest real faith actually at work is better than the best ideal of it left in the region of speculation. The great matter is to believe on the Lord Jesus at once. Never mind distinctions and definitions. A hungry man eats even though he does not understand the composition of his food, the anatomy of his mouth, or the process of his digestion. He knows that he lives because he eats. Another far more clever person understands thoroughly the science of nutrition, but if he does not eat, he will die with all his knowledge. There are, no doubt, many in hell at this hour who understood the doctrine of faith but did not believe. On the other hand, not one who has trusted in the Lord Jesus has ever been cast out, though he may never have been able to intelligently define his faith. Oh, receive the Lord Jesus into your soul, and you will live forever! *"He that believeth on the Son hath everlasting life"* (John 3:36).

Chapter 9
How May Faith Be Illustrated?

Faith is the substance of things hoped for,
the evidence of things not seen.
—Hebrews 11:1

I will give you a few illustrations to make the matter of faith clearer. Though the Holy Spirit alone can make you see, it is my duty and my joy to furnish all the light I can and to pray to the divine Lord to open blind eyes. Oh, that you would pray the same prayer for yourself!

Faith Illustrated by the Human Body

The Eye

The faith that saves has its analogies in the human body. It is the *eye* that looks. The eye brings into the mind what is far away. We can bring the sun and the far-off stars into the mind by a glance of the eye. So by trust we bring the Lord Jesus near to us. And though He is far away in heaven, He enters into our hearts. Only look to Jesus, for the hymn is exactly true:

> There is life in a look at the Crucified One,
> There is life at this moment for thee.

The Hand

Faith is the *hand* that grasps. When a hand takes hold of anything for itself, it does precisely what faith does when it appropriates Christ and the blessings of His redemption. Faith says, "Jesus is mine." Faith hears of the pardoning blood and cries, "I accept it to pardon *me*." Faith calls the legacies of the dying Jesus its own. And they are faith's own, for faith is Christ's heir; He has given Himself and all that He has to faith. Take what grace has provided for you. You will not be a thief, for you have a divine permit: *"Whosoever will, let him take the water of life freely"* (Revelation 22:17). He who may have a treasure simply by grasping it will be foolish indeed if he remains poor.

The Mouth

Faith is the *mouth* that feeds on Christ. Before food can nourish us, it must be received into us. This eating and drinking is a simple matter. We willingly receive food into our mouths, and then we allow it to pass down into our inward parts where it is taken up and absorbed into our bodily frames. Paul said in Romans 10:8, *"The word is nigh thee, even in thy mouth."* Now all that is left to be done is to swallow it, to allow it to go down into the soul. Oh, that men had an appetite! For he who is hungry and sees meat before him does not need to be taught how to eat. "Give me," said one, "a knife and a fork and a chance." He was fully prepared to do the rest. A heart that truly hungers and thirsts after Christ only has to know that He is freely given and at once it will receive Him. If you are in such a case, do not hesitate to receive Jesus. You may be sure that you will never be blamed for doing so, for *"as many as received him, to them gave he power to become the sons of God"* (John 1:12). He never rejects anyone, but He authorizes all who come to remain sons forever.

Faith Illustrated by the Pursuits of Life

The pursuits of life illustrate faith in many ways. The farmer buries good seed in the earth and expects it not only to live but also to multiply. He has faith in the covenant arrangement that *"seedtime and harvest...shall not cease"* (Genesis 8:22). He is rewarded for his faith.

The merchant places his money in the care of a banker and completely trusts the honesty and soundness of the bank. He entrusts his capital to another's hands and feels far more at ease than if he had the solid gold locked up in an iron safe.

The sailor trusts himself to the sea. When he swims, he lifts his feet from the bottom and rests on the buoyant ocean. He could not swim if he did not wholly cast himself upon the water.

The goldsmith puts precious metal into the fire, which seems eager to consume it. However, he receives it back again from the furnace purified by the heat.

You cannot turn anywhere in life without seeing faith in operation between man and man or between man and natural law. Now, just as we trust in daily life, even so are we to trust in God as He is revealed in Christ Jesus.

Faith Illustrated by Its Degrees

Faith exists in different persons in various degrees, according to the amount of their knowledge or growth in grace.

Clinging Faith

Sometimes faith is little more than a simple *clinging* to Christ—a sense of dependence and a willingness to depend. When you are down at the seashore, you will see limpets sticking to the rocks. You can walk softly up to a rock, strike a mollusk a quick blow with a stick, and off he comes. Yet try the next limpet in that way. You have given him warning; he heard the blow with which you struck his neighbor, and he clings with all his might. You will never get him off! Strike and strike again, but you might as well break the rock. The limpet does not know much, but he clings. He is not acquainted with the geological formation of the rock, but he clings. He can cling and has found something to cling to; this is all his stock of knowledge, and he uses it for his security and salvation. It is the limpet's life to cling to the rock, and it is the sinner's life to cling to Jesus. Thousands of God's people have no more faith than this. They know enough to cling to Jesus with all their heart and soul, and this suffices for present peace and eternal safety. Jesus Christ is to them a strong and mighty Savior, a Rock immovable and immutable. They cling to Him for dear life, and this clinging saves them. Can you not cling? Do so at once.

Faith That Trusts in Jesus' Merits and Truth

Another example of faith is when one man relies on another because of a knowledge of the superiority of the other. This is a higher faith—the faith that knows the reason for its dependence and acts on it. I do not think the limpet knows much about the rock, but, as faith grows, it becomes more and more intelligent. A blind man trusts himself with his guide because he knows that his friend can see. Trusting, he walks where his guide conducts him. If the poor man is born blind, he does not know what sight is, but he knows that there is such a thing as sight and that it is possessed by his friend. Therefore, he freely puts his hand into the hand of the seeing one and follows his leadership. *"We walk by faith, not by sight"* (2 Corinthians 5:7). *"Blessed are they that have not seen, and yet have believed"* (John 20:29). This is an excellent image of faith. We know that Jesus has merit and power and blessing that we do not possess, and therefore we gladly trust Him to be to us what we cannot be to ourselves. We trust Him as the blind man trusts his guide. He never betrays our confidence, but He becomes "[for] *us wisdom, and righteousness, and sanctification, and redemption"* (1 Corinthians 1:30).

Every child who goes to school has to exert faith while learning. His teacher teaches him geography and instructs him as to the form of the earth and the existence of certain great cities and empires. The child himself does not know that these things are true, except that he believes his teacher and the books put into his hands. That is what you will have to do with Christ if you are to be saved. You must simply know because He tells you, believe because He assures you it is so, and trust yourself with Him because He promises you that salvation will be the result.

Almost all that you and I know has come to us by faith. A scientific discovery has been made, and we are sure of it. On what grounds do we believe it? On the authority of certain well-known men of learning whose reputations are established. We have never made or seen their experiments, but we believe their witness. You must do the same with regard to Jesus. Because He teaches you certain truths, you are to be His disciples and believe His words. Because He has performed certain acts, you are to be His clients and trust yourselves with Him. He is infinitely superior to you and presents Himself to you as your Master and Lord. If you will receive Him and His words, you will be saved.

Faith That Grows out of Love

Another and a higher form of faith is the faith that grows out of love. Why does a child trust his father? It is because he loves him. Blessed and happy are they who have a sweet faith in Jesus intertwined with deep affection for Him, for this is a restful confidence. These lovers of Jesus are enthralled with His character and delighted with His mission. They are carried away by the lovingkindness that He has manifested. Therefore, they cannot help trusting Him because they so much admire, revere, and love Him.

The way of loving trust in the Savior is illustrated by a lady who is the wife of the most eminent physician of the day. She is seized with a dangerous illness and is afflicted by its power. Yet she is wonderfully calm and quiet because her husband has made this disease his special study and has healed thousands who were similarly afflicted. She is not in the least troubled, for she feels perfectly safe in the hands of one so dear to her and in whom skill and love are blended in their highest forms. Her faith is reasonable and natural; her husband, from every point of view, deserves it from her.

This is the kind of faith that the happiest of believers exercise toward Christ. There is no physician like Him; none can save as He can. We love Him, and He loves us. Therefore, we put ourselves into His hands, accept whatever He prescribes, and do whatever He bids. We feel that nothing can be wrongly ordered while He is the Director of our affairs. He loves us too well to let us perish or suffer a single needless pang.

Faith is the root of obedience, and this truth may be clearly seen in the affairs of life. When a captain trusts a pilot to steer his vessel into port, he manages the vessel according to his direction. When a traveler trusts a guide to conduct him over a difficult pass, he follows the track that his guide points out. When a patient believes in a physician, he carefully follows his prescriptions and directions. Faith that refuses to obey the commands of the Savior is a mere pretense and will never save the soul. We trust Jesus to save us. He gives us directions as to the way of salvation; we follow those directions and are saved. Do not forget this. Trust Jesus and prove your trust by doing whatever He bids you.

Faith That Arises from Assured Knowledge

A notable form of faith rises out of assured knowledge. This comes by growth in grace and is the faith that believes Christ because it knows Him. It trusts Christ because it has proven Him to be infallibly faithful. An old Christian was in the habit of writing *T* and *P* in the margin of her Bible whenever she had tried and proven a promise. How easy it is to trust a tried and proven Savior! You may not do this as yet, but you will do so. Everything must have a beginning. You will rise to strong faith in due time. This matured faith does not ask for signs and tokens, but bravely believes.

Look at the faith of the master mariner; I have often wondered at it. He loosens his cable and steams away from the land. For days, weeks, or even months, he never sees sail or shore. Yet on he goes, day and night, without fear until one morning he finds himself closely approaching the desired haven toward which he has been steering. How has he found his way over the trackless deep? He has trusted in his compass, his nautical almanac, his glass, and the heavenly bodies. Obeying their guidance, without sighting land, he has steered so accurately that he has not had to change a point to enter into port. It is a wonderful thing to sail or steam without sight.

Spiritually, it is a blessed thing to altogether leave the shores of sight and feeling and to say good-bye to inward feelings, cheering providences, signs, tokens, and so forth. It is glorious to be far out on the ocean of divine love, believing in God and steering straight for heaven by the direction of the Word of God. *"Blessed are they that have not seen, and yet have believed"* (John 20:29). A safe voyage on the way and an abundant entrance at the last will be given to them. Will you put your trust in God, in Christ Jesus? There I rest with joyous confidence. Come with me and believe our Father and our Savior. Come at once.

Chapter 10
Why Are We Saved by Faith?

For by grace are ye saved through faith; and that not of yourselves: it is the gift of God.
—Ephesians 2:8

Why is faith selected as the channel of salvation? No doubt this inquiry is often made. *"By grace are ye saved **through faith**"* is assuredly the doctrine of Holy Scripture and the ordinance of God, but why is this so? Why is faith selected rather than hope or love or patience?

Faith Is Naturally Adapted as the Receiver

It becomes us to be modest in answering such a question. God's ways are not always to be understood, nor are we allowed to presumptuously question them. Humbly we would reply that, as far as we can tell, faith has been selected as the channel of grace because faith is naturally adapted to be used as the receiver. Suppose that I am about to give a poor man some money. I will put it into his hand. Why? Well, it would hardly be fitting to put it into his ear or to lay it on his foot. The hand seems made on purpose to receive. So, in our mental frame, faith is created on purpose to be a receiver. It is like the hand of a man, and there is a fitness in receiving grace by its means.

Let me put this very plainly. Receiving Christ by faith is as simple an act as when your child receives an apple from you because you hold it out and promise to give him the apple if he comes for it. The belief and the receiving relate only to an apple, but they make up precisely the same act as the faith that deals with eternal salvation. What the child's hand is to the apple, your faith is to the perfect salvation of Christ. The child's hand does not make the apple nor improve the apple nor deserve the apple; it only takes it. And faith is chosen by God to be the receiver of salvation because it does not pretend to create salvation or to help in it, but is content to receive it humbly. "Faith is the tongue that begs pardon, the hand that receives it, and the eye that sees it; but it is not the price that buys it." Faith never makes itself its own plea. It rests all its argument on the blood of Christ. It becomes a good servant to bring the riches of the Lord Jesus to the soul because it acknowledges from where it drew them and admits that grace alone entrusted it with them.

Faith Gives All the Glory to God

Faith is again selected because it gives all the glory to God. *"It is of faith, that it might be by grace"* (Romans 4:16), and it is of grace that there might be no boasting, for God cannot endure pride. *"The proud he knoweth afar off"* (Psalm 138:6). He has no wish to come nearer to them. He will not give salvation in a way that will suggest or foster pride. Paul said, *"Not of works, lest any man should boast"* (Ephesians 2:9). Now, faith excludes all boasting. The hand that receives charity does not say, "I am to be thanked for accepting the gift"; that would be absurd. When the hand gives bread to the mouth, it does not say to the body, "Thank me, for I feed you." It is a very simple thing that the hand does—though very necessary—and it never designates glory to itself for what it does. So God has selected faith to receive the *"unspeakable gift"* (2 Corinthians 9:15) of His grace. It cannot take any credit to itself but must adore the gracious God who is the Giver of all good. Faith sets the crown on the right head. Therefore, the Lord Jesus was accustomed to putting the crown on the head of faith, saying, *"Thy faith hath saved thee; go in peace"* (Luke 7:50).

Faith Is a Sure Method of Linking Man with God

Next, God selects faith as the channel of salvation because it is a sure method of linking man with God. When man confides in God, there is a point of union between them, and that union guarantees blessing. Faith saves us because it makes us cling to God and therefore connects us with Him. I have often used the following illustration. Years ago, a boat was upset above Niagara Falls. Two men were being carried down the current when people on the shore managed to float a rope out to them. Both seized it. One of them held on to it and was safely drawn to the bank. However, the other, seeing a great log come floating by, unwisely let go of the rope and clung to the log, for it was bigger and apparently better to cling to. The log with the man on it went right over the vast abyss because nothing connected the log and the shore. The size of the log was of no benefit to him who grasped it; it needed a connection with the shore to produce safety.

So when a man trusts to his works or to sacraments or to anything of that sort, he will not be saved, because there is no junction between him and Christ. However, faith, though it may seem to be like a slender cord, is in the hands of the great God on the shore. Infinite power pulls in the connecting line between God and faith and thus draws the man from destruction. Oh, the blessedness of faith because it ties us to God!

Faith Touches the Springs of Action

Faith is chosen again because it touches the springs of action. Even in common things, faith of a certain sort lies at the root of all. I wonder whether I am wrong if I say that we never do anything except through faith of some sort. If I walk across my study, it is because I believe my legs will carry me. A man eats because he believes in the necessity of food. He goes to his business because he believes in the value of money. He accepts a check because he believes that the bank will honor it. Colombus discovered America because he believed that there was another continent beyond the ocean. The Pilgrim fathers colonized it because they believed that God would be with them on those rocky shores. Most grand deeds have been born of faith. For good or for evil, faith works wonders by the person in whom it dwells.

Faith in its natural form is an all-prevailing force that enters into all manner of human actions. Possibly he who mocks faith in God is the man who in an evil form has the most faith.

Indeed, he usually falls into a credulity that would be ridiculous if it were not disgraceful. God gives salvation to faith, because by creating faith in us He thus touches the real mainspring of our emotions and actions. He has, so to speak, taken possession of the battery, and now He can send the sacred current to every part of our nature. When we believe in Christ, and the heart has come into the possession of God, then we are saved from sin and are moved toward repentance, holiness, zeal, prayer, consecration, and every other gracious thing. "What oil is to the wheels, what weights are to a clock, what wings are to a bird, what sails are to a ship, faith is to all holy duties and services." Have faith, and all other graces will follow and continue to hold their course.

Faith Draws the Heart to God

Faith, again, has the power of working by love (Galatians 5:6). It influences the affections toward God and draws the heart after the best things. He who believes in God will beyond all question love God. Faith is an act of understanding, but it also proceeds from the heart. *"With the heart man believeth unto righteousness"* (Romans 10:10). Hence, God gives salvation to faith because it resides next door to the affections and is closely related to love. And love is the parent and the nurse of every holy feeling and act. Love for God is obedience; love for God is holiness. To love God and to love man is to be conformed to the image of Christ, and this is salvation.

Faith Creates Peace and Joy

Moreover, faith creates peace and joy. He who has it rests and is tranquil, glad, and joyous, and this is a preparation for heaven. God gives all heavenly gifts to faith for this reason, among others: Faith works in us the life and spirit that are to be eternally manifested in the upper and better world. Faith furnishes us with armor for this life and education for the life to come. It enables a man both to live and to die without fear; it prepares both for action and for suffering. Hence, the Lord selects it as a most convenient medium for conveying grace to us and thereby securing us for glory.

Certainly, faith does for us what nothing else can do. It gives us joy and peace and causes us to enter into rest. Why do men attempt to gain salvation by other means? An old preacher said,

> A silly servant, who is told to open a door, puts his shoulder against it and pushes with all his might, but the door does not stir, and he cannot enter, whatever strength he uses. Another comes with a key, easily unlocks the door, and enters immediately. Those who would be saved by works are pushing at heaven's gate

without result, but faith is the key that opens the gate at once.

Will you not use that key? The Lord commands you to believe in His dear Son. Therefore, you may do so, and in doing so you will live. Is this not the promise of the Gospel: *"He that believeth and is baptized shall be saved"* (Mark 16:16)? What can your objection be to a way of salvation that commends itself to the mercy and the wisdom of our gracious God?

Chapter 11

I Can Do Nothing!

When we were yet without strength,
in due time Christ died for the ungodly.
—Romans 5:6

*A*fter the anxious heart has accepted the doctrine of atonement and learned the great truth that salvation is by faith in the Lord Jesus, it is often troubled with a sense of inability toward that which is good. Many are groaning, "I can do nothing." They are not using this as an excuse, but they feel it as a daily burden. They would if they could. Each one can honestly say, *"To will is present with me; but how to perform that which is good I find not"* (Romans 7:18).

This feeling seems to make all the Gospel null and void, for what is the use of food to a hungry man if he cannot get at it? Of what avail is the river of the water of life if one cannot drink? There is a story of a doctor and a poor woman's child. The learned practitioner told the mother that her little one would soon be better under proper treatment, but it was absolutely necessary that her boy regularly drink the best wine and spend a season at one of the German spas. This he said to a widow who could hardly get enough bread to eat! Now, it sometimes seems to the troubled heart that the simple Gospel of "Believe and live" is not, after all, so very simple. It asks the poor sinner to do what he cannot do. To the suddenly awakened but half-instructed person, there appears to be a missing link. Yonder is the salvation of Jesus, but how is it to be reached? The soul is without strength and does not know what to do. It lies within sight of the city of refuge, but cannot enter its gate.

Is this lack of strength provided for in the plan of salvation? It is. The work of the Lord is perfect. It begins where we are and asks nothing of us for its completion. When the Good Samaritan saw the traveler lying wounded and half dead, he did not tell him to rise and come to him, mount the donkey, and ride off to the inn. No, he *"went to him"* (Luke 10:34) and ministered to him. He lifted him up onto the animal and took him to the inn. Thus does the Lord Jesus deal with us in our low and wretched state.

I Can Do Nothing!

We have seen that God justifies, that He *"justifieth the ungodly"* (Romans 4:5), and that He justifies them through faith in the precious blood of Jesus. We now have to see the condition these ungodly ones are in when Jesus works out their salvation. Many people who are newly awakened are troubled not only about their sin, but also about their moral weakness. They have no strength with which to escape from the mire into which they have fallen or to keep out of it in the days to come. They lament not only over what they have done, but also over what they cannot do. They feel powerless, helpless, and spiritually lifeless. It may sound odd to say that they feel dead, yet it is so. They are, in their own opinion, incapable of all good. They cannot travel the road to heaven, for their bones are broken. *"None of the men of might* [strength] *have found their hands"* (Psalm 76:5). In fact, they are *"without strength."* Happily, this truth is written as the commendation of God's love to us: *"When we were yet without strength, in due time Christ died for the ungodly."*

Here we see conscious helplessness helped by the interposition of the Lord Jesus. Our helplessness is extreme. It is not written, "When we were comparatively weak, Christ died for us," or "When we had only a little strength," but the description is absolute and unrestricted: *"When we were yet without strength."* We have no strength whatsoever that can aid in our salvation. Our Lord's words are emphatically true: *"Without me ye can do nothing"* (John 15:5). I will go further than the text and remind you of the great love with which the Lord loved us even when we *"were dead in trespasses and sins"* (Ephesians 2:1). To be dead is even worse than being without strength.

The one thing that the poor strengthless sinner has to fix his mind on and firmly retain as his one ground of hope is the divine assurance that *"in due time Christ died for the ungodly."* Believe this, and all inability will disappear. As it is fabled of Midas that he turned everything into gold by his touch, so it is true of faith that it turns everything it touches into good. Our very needs and weaknesses become blessings when faith deals with them.

Forms of Lack of Strength

Weakness in Thinking and Concentration

Let us consider certain forms of this lack of strength. To begin with, one man will say, "Sir, I do not seem to have the strength to collect my thoughts and keep them fixed on those solemn topics that concern my salvation. A short prayer is almost too much for me. It is partly so, perhaps, through natural weakness, partly because I have injured myself through excessive drinking, and partly because I worry myself with worldly cares so that I am not capable of those high thoughts that are necessary before a soul can be saved."

This is a very common form of sinful weakness. Note this! You are without strength on this point, and there are many like you. They could not carry out a train of consecutive thought to save their lives. Many poor men and women are illiterate and untrained, and they find deep thought to be very hard work. Others are so light and trifling by nature that they could no more follow out a long process of argument and reasoning than they could fly. They could never attain to the knowledge of any profound mystery if they spent their whole life in the effort.

You need not, therefore, despair. What is necessary to salvation is not continuous thought but a simple reliance upon Jesus. Hold onto this one fact: *"In due time Christ died for the ungodly."* This truth will not require you to do any deep research or profound reasoning or convincing argument. There it stands: *"In due time Christ died for the ungodly."*

Fix your mind on that, and rest there. Let this one great, gracious, glorious fact lie in your spirit until it permeates all your thoughts and makes you rejoice even though you are without strength. Rejoice that the Lord Jesus has become your strength and your song; yes, He has become your salvation (Exodus 15:2). According to the Scriptures, it is a revealed fact that *"in due time*

Christist died for the ungodly" when they were *"yet without strength."* Maybe you have heard these words hundreds of times, and yet you have never before perceived their meaning. There is a wonderful thing about them. Jesus did not die for our righteousness, but He died for our sins. He did not come to save us because we were worth saving, but because we were utterly worthless, ruined, and undone. He did not come to earth out of any reason that was in us, but solely and only because of reasons that He took from the depths of His own divine love.

In due time Jesus died for those whom He describes not as godly but as *"ungodly,"* describing them with as hopeless an adjective as He could have selected. Even if you think little, fasten your mind to this truth, for it is fitted to the smallest capacity and is able to cheer the heaviest heart. Let this text lie under your tongue like a sweet morsel until it dissolves into your heart and flavors all your thoughts. People who have never shone in science nor displayed the least originality of thinking have nevertheless been fully able to accept the doctrine of the Cross and have been saved. Why should you not?

Inability to Repent

I hear another man cry, "Oh, sir, my lack of strength lies mainly in that I cannot repent sufficiently!" What a curious idea men have of what repentance is! Many believe that so many tears are to be shed and so many groans are to be heaved and so much despair is to be endured. Where do they get this unreasonable notion? Unbelief and despair are sins. Therefore, I do not see how they can be constituent elements of acceptable repentance. Yet there are many who regard them as necessary parts of true Christian experience. They are in great error.

Still, I know what they mean, for in the days of my darkness, I used to feel the same way. I desired to repent, but I thought that I could not do it. Yet, all the while, I was repenting. Odd as it may sound, I felt that I could not feel. I used to get into a corner and weep because I could not weep. I was bitterly sorrowful because I could not sorrow for sin. What a jumble it all is when in our unbelieving state we begin to judge our own condition! It is like a blind man looking at his own eyes. My heart was melted within me for fear because I thought that my heart was as hard as stone. My heart was broken to think that it would not break. Now I can see that I was exhibiting the very thing that I thought I did not possess; but *then* I did not know where I was.

Oh, that I could help others into the light that I now enjoy! I would gladly say a word that might shorten the time of their bewilderment. I would say a few plain words and ask the Comforter to apply them to the heart.

Remember that the man who truly repents is never satisfied with his own repentance. We can no more repent perfectly than we can live perfectly. However pure our tears, there will always be some dirt in them; there will be something to be repented of even in our best repentance. Yet listen! To repent is to change your mind about sin and Christ and all the great things of God. There is sorrow implied in this, but the main point is the turning of the heart from sin to Christ. If there is this turning, you have the essence of true repentance, even though no alarm and no despair have ever cast their shadow on your mind.

If you find it difficult to repent, it will greatly help you to firmly believe that *"in due time Christ died for the ungodly."* Think of this again and again. How can you continue to be hardhearted when you know that out of supreme love *"Christ died for the ungodly"*? Let me persuade you to reason with yourself like this: "Ungodly as I am, though this heart of steel will not relent, though I hit my chest in vain, yet He died for such as I am, because He died for the ungodly. Oh, that I may believe this and feel the power of it in my unmerciful heart!"

Blot out every other reflection from your soul; sit down by the hour and meditate deeply on this one resplendent display of unmerited, unexpected, unparalleled love: *"Christ died for the ungodly."* Carefully read over the narrative of the Lord's

death as you find it in the four Gospels. If anything can melt your stubborn heart, it will be a
view of the sufferings of Jesus and the knowledge
that He suffered all this for His enemies.

> O Jesus, sweet the tears I shed,
>   While at Thy cross I kneel,
> Gaze on Thy wounded, fainting head,
>   And all Thy sorrows feel.
>
> My heart dissolves to see Thee bleed,
>   This heart so hard before;
> I hear Thee for the guilty plead,
>   And grief o'erflows the more.
>
> ' Twas for the sinful Thou didst die,
>   And I a sinner stand:
> Convinc'd by Thine expiring eye,
>   Slain by Thy piercèd hand.
>   —Ray Palmer

Surely, the Cross is that wonder-working rod
that can bring water out of a rock. If you understand the full meaning of the divine sacrifice
of Jesus, you must repent of ever having been
opposed to One who is so full of love. It is written, *"They shall look upon me whom they have
pierced, and they shall mourn for him, as one
mourneth for his only son, and shall be in bitterness for him, as one that is in bitterness for his
firstborn"* (Zechariah 12:10). Repentance will not
make you see Christ, but to see Christ will give

you repentance. You may not make a christ out of your repentance, but you must look to Christ for repentance. The Holy Spirit, by turning us to Christ, turns us from sin. Look away, then, from the effect to the cause, from your own repenting to the Lord Jesus, who is exalted on high to give repentance.

Tormenting and Blasphemous Thoughts

I have heard another say, "I am tormented with horrible thoughts. Wherever I go, blasphemies steal in on me. Frequently, at my work, a dreadful suggestion forces itself upon me. Even in my bed, I am startled from my sleep by whispers of the evil one. I cannot get away from this horrible temptation." Friend, I know what you mean, for I myself have been hunted by this wolf. A man might as well hope to fight a swarm of flies with a sword as to master his own thoughts when they are set on by the devil. A poor tempted soul, assailed by satanic suggestions, is like a traveler I have read about. His head and ears and whole body were attacked by a swarm of angry bees. He could not keep them off or escape from them. They stung him everywhere and threatened to kill him. I do not wonder that you feel that you have no strength to stop these hideous and abominable thoughts that Satan pours into your soul. Yet I would remind you of the Scripture before us: *"When we were yet without strength, in due time Christ died for the ungodly."*

I Can Do Nothing!

Jesus knew where we were and where we should be. He saw that we could not overcome *"the prince of the power of the air"* (Ephesians 2:2). He knew that we would be greatly worried by the devil. Yet, even then, when He saw us in that condition, Christ died for the ungodly. Cast the anchor of your faith on this. The devil himself cannot tell you that you are not ungodly.

Believe, then, that Jesus died even for such as you are. Remember Martin Luther's way of cutting the devil's head off with his own sword. "Oh," said the devil to Martin Luther, "you are a sinner." "Yes," said Luther, "Christ died to save sinners." Thus he smote him with his own sword. Hide in this refuge and stay there: *"In due time Christ died for the ungodly."* If you stand on that truth, your blasphemous thoughts, which you do not have the strength to drive away, will go away by themselves, for Satan will see that he is achieving nothing by plaguing you with them.

These thoughts, if you hate them, are not yours but are injections of the devil. He is responsible, and not you. If you strive against them, they are no more yours than are the cursings and false-hoods of rioters in the street. It is by means of these thoughts that the devil wants to drive you to despair, or at least keep you from trusting Jesus. The poor diseased woman could not come to Jesus because of the crowd. You are in much the same condition because of the rush and crowd of these dreadful thoughts. Still, she put forth her finger and touched the fringe of the Lord's garment, and she was healed. (See Mark 5:25–34.) Do the same.

Jesus died for those who are guilty of *"all manner of sin and blasphemy"* (Matthew 12:31). Therefore, I am sure He will not refuse those who are unwillingly the captives of evil thoughts. Cast yourself upon Him, thoughts and all, and prove that He is mighty to save. He can still those horrible whisperings of the fiend, or He can enable you to see them in their true light so that you will not be worried by them. In His own way, He can and will save you and, at length, give you perfect peace. Only trust Him for this and everything else.

Lack of Power to Believe

The form of inability that lies in a supposed lack of power to believe is sadly perplexing. We are not strangers to the cry,

> Oh, that I could believe,
>   Then all would easy be;
> I would, but cannot; Lord, relieve,
>   My help must come from Thee.

Many remain in the dark for years because they have no strength, they say, to give up all power and rest in the power of Another, the Lord Jesus. Indeed, this whole matter of believing is a very curious thing, for people do not get much help by trying to believe. Believing does not come by trying. If a person were to make a statement of something that happened today, I would not tell him that I would *try* to believe him. If I believed in the truthfulness of the man who told me the incident and said that he saw it, I would accept the statement at once. If I did not think he was a truthful man, I would, of course, disbelieve him. There would be no *trying* in the matter. Now, when God declares that there is salvation in Christ Jesus, I must either believe Him at once or call Him a liar. Surely, you will not hesitate as to which is the right path in this case. The witness of God must be true, and we are bound at once to believe in Jesus.

Yet possibly you have been trying to believe too much. Do not aim at great things. Be satisfied to have a faith that can hold in its hand this one truth: *"When we were yet without strength, in due time Christ died for the ungodly."* He laid down His life for men while they were not yet believing in Him, nor were able to believe in Him. He died for men, not as believers but as sinners. He came to make these sinners into believers and saints, but when He died for them, He viewed them as utterly without strength. If you believe that Christ died for the ungodly, your faith will save you, and you may go in peace. If you will trust your soul to Jesus, who died for the ungodly, even though you cannot believe all things or move mountains or do any other wonderful works, yet you will be saved. It is not great faith but true faith that saves. Salvation lies not in the faith but in the Christ in whom faith trusts. Faith as a grain of mustard seed will bring salvation. It is not the amount of faith but the sincerity of faith that is the point to be considered. Surely, a man can believe what he knows to be true; and as you know Jesus to be true, you can believe in Him.

The cross, which is the object of faith, is also, by the power of the Holy Spirit, the cause of it. Sit down and watch the dying Savior until faith springs up spontaneously in your heart. There is no place like Calvary for creating confidence. The air of that sacred hill brings health to trembling faith. Many a watcher there has said,

> While I view Thee, wounded, grieving,
> Breathless on the cursèd tree,
> Lord, I feel my heart believing
> That Thou suffer'dst thus for me.

Inability to Stop Sinning

"Alas!" cries another, "my trouble is that I cannot quit my sinning. I know that I cannot go to heaven and carry my sin with me." I am glad that you know that, for it is quite true. You must be divorced from your sin, or you cannot be married to Christ. Recall the question that flashed into the mind of young Bunyan while he was playing sports on Sunday: "Wilt thou have thy sins and go to hell, or wilt thou quit thy sins and go to heaven?" That brought him to a dead stop. That is a question that every man will have to answer, for there is no going on in sin and going to heaven. That cannot be. You must quit sin or quit hope.

Do you reply, "Yes, I am willing enough. *'To will is present with me; but how to perform that which* [I would] *I find not'* (Romans 7:18). Sin masters me, and I have no strength." Come, then, if you have no strength; this text is still true: *"When we were yet without strength, in due time Christ died for the ungodly."* Can you still believe that? No matter how many other things may seem to contradict it, will you still believe it? God has said it, and it is a fact; therefore, hold on to it tightly, for your only hope lies there. Believe this, trust Jesus, and you will soon find power with which to slay your sin. However, apart from Him, the armed strongman will hold you forever as his bondslave.

Personally, I could never have overcome my own sinfulness. I tried and failed. My evil tendencies were too much for me until, in the belief that Christ died for me, I cast my guilty soul on Him. And then I received a conquering principle by which I overcame my sinful self. The doctrine of the Cross can be used to slay sin as the old warriors used their huge two-handed swords and mowed down their foes at every stroke. There is nothing like faith in the sinner's Friend; it overcomes all evil. If Christ has died for me—ungodly as I am, without strength as I am—then I can no longer live in sin, but must rouse myself to love and serve Him who has redeemed me. I cannot trifle with the evil that slew my Best Friend. I must be holy for His sake. How can I live in sin when He has died to save me from it?

See what a splendid help this is to you who are without strength—to know and believe that in due time Christ died for such ungodly ones as you are. Have you caught the idea yet? It is, somehow, so difficult for our darkened, prejudiced, and unbelieving minds to see the essence of the Gospel. At times I have thought, when I have finished preaching, that I have presented the Gospel so clearly that the nose on one's face could not be more plain. Yet I perceive that even intelligent hearers have failed to understand what was meant by *"Look unto me, and be ye saved"* (Isaiah 45:22). Converts usually say that they did not know the Gospel until such and such a day, yet they had heard it for years. The Gospel is unknown, not from lack of explanation, but from absence of personal revelation. This the Holy Spirit is ready to give and will give to those who ask Him. Yet, when given, the sum total of the truth revealed lies within these words: *"Christ died for the ungodly."*

The Fear of Man

I hear another person bewailing himself thus: "Oh, sir, my weakness lies in this: I do not seem to keep spiritual things in my mind long! I hear the Word on a Sunday, and I am impressed. Yet, during the week, I meet with an evil companion, and my good feelings are all gone. My fellow workmen do not believe in anything, and they say such terrible things. I do not know how to answer them, so I find myself knocked over." I know this Plastic Pliable very well, and I tremble for him. However, at the same time, if he is really sincere, his weakness can be met by divine grace. The Holy Spirit can cast out the evil spirit of the fear of man. He can make the coward brave.

Remember, my poor vacillating friend, you must not remain in this state. It will never do to be mean and beggarly to yourself. Stand upright and look at yourself. See if you were ever meant to be like a toad under a rotary cultivator, afraid for your life either to move or to stand still. Do have a mind of your own.

This is not a spiritual matter only, but one that concerns ordinary human nature. I would do many things to please my friends, but to go to hell to please them is more than I would venture. It may be very well to do this and that for good fellowship, but it will never do to lose the friendship of God in order to keep on good terms with men. "I know that," says the man, "but still, though I know it, I cannot get enough courage. I cannot show my colors. I cannot stand fast." Well, to you, also, I have the same text to bring: *"When we were yet without strength, in due time Christ died for the ungodly."*

If Peter were here, he would say, "The Lord Jesus died for me even when I was such a poor weak creature that the maid who kept the fire drove me to lie and to swear that I did not know the Lord." (See Matthew 26:69–74.) Yes, Jesus died for those who forsook Him and fled. Take a firm grip on this truth: Christ died for the ungodly while they were yet without strength. This is your way out of your cowardice. Get this thought, "Christ died for me," worked into your soul, and you will soon be ready to die for Him. Believe that He suffered in your stead and offered for you a full, true, and satisfactory atonement. If you believe that fact, you will be forced to feel, "I cannot be ashamed of Him who died for me." A full conviction that this is true will give you fearless courage.

Look at the saints in the martyr age. In the early days of Christianity, when this great thought of Christ's exceeding love was sparkling in all its freshness in the church, men were not only ready to die, but also grew ambitious to suffer and even presented themselves by the hundreds at the judgment seats of the rulers, confessing the Christ. I do not say that they were wise to court a cruel death, but it proves my point that a sense of the love of Jesus lifts the mind above all fear of what man can do to us. Why should it not produce this effect in you? Oh, that it might now inspire you with a brave resolve to come out on the Lord's side and be His follower to the end!

May the Holy Spirit help us to come thus far by faith in the Lord Jesus, and it will be well!

Chapter 12
The Increase of Faith

The apostles said unto the Lord,
Increase our faith.
—Luke 17:5

How can we increase our faith? This is a very earnest question for many. They say they want to believe but cannot. A great deal of nonsense is said about this subject. Let us be strictly practical in our dealing with it. Common sense is as much needed in Christianity as anywhere else.

Ways to Increase Faith

Believe at Once

"What am I to do in order to believe?" One who was asked the best way to do a certain simple act replied that the best way to do it was to do it at once. We waste time in discussing methods when the action is simple. The shortest way to believe is to believe. If the Holy Spirit has made you candid, you will believe as soon as truth is set before you. You will believe it because it is true. The Gospel command is clear, *"Believe on the Lord Jesus Christ, and thou shalt be saved"* (Acts 16:31). It is idle to evade this truth by questions and quibbles. The order is clear; let it be obeyed.

Ask God to Lead You into the Truth

Yet still, if you have difficulty, take it before God in prayer. Tell God the Father exactly what it is that puzzles you, and beg Him by His Holy Spirit to solve the question. If I cannot believe a statement in a book, I ask the author what he means by it. If he is an honest man, his explanation will satisfy me. The divine explanation of the hard points of Scripture will satisfy the heart of the true seeker much more than this. The Lord is willing to make Himself known. Go to Him and see if it is not so. Go at once to prayer and cry, "O Holy Spirit, lead me into the truth! Teach me what I do not know."

Hear the Gospel Often and Attentively

Furthermore, if faith seems difficult, it is possible that God the Holy Spirit will enable you to believe if you listen often and well to what you are commanded to believe. We believe many things because we have heard them so often. Do you not find that, in everyday life, if you hear a thing fifty times a day, you come to believe it? Some men have come to believe very unlikely statements by this process. Therefore, I can easily understand why the Holy Spirit often blesses this method of hearing the truth and uses it to work faith concerning what is to be believed. It is written, *"Faith cometh by hearing"* (Romans 10:17). Therefore, hear often. If I earnestly and attentively hear the Gospel, one of these days I will find myself believing it because of the blessed workings of the Spirit of God on my mind. Only, be sure you hear the Gospel, and do not be distracted by either hearing or reading what is designed to make you doubt.

Consider the Testimony of Others

If that should seem to be poor advice, I would add this next: Consider the testimony of others. The Samaritans believed because of what the woman told them concerning Jesus. (See John 4:6–30, 39.) Many of our beliefs arise out of the testimony of others. I believe that there is such a country as Japan. I have never seen it, yet I believe that there is such a place because others have been there. I believe that I will die. I have never died, but a great many people whom I once knew have died. Therefore, I believe that I will also die. The experience of many convinces me of that fact.

All of Grace

Listen, then, to those who tell you how they were saved, how they were pardoned, how they were changed in character. If you will look into the matter, you will find that somebody just like yourself has been saved. If you have been a thief, you will find that a thief rejoiced to wash away his sin in the fountain of Christ's blood. If, unhappily, you have been unchaste, you will find that men and women who have fallen in that way have been cleansed and changed. If you are in despair, you need only to get among God's people and inquire a little. You will discover that some of the saints have been equally in despair at times. They will be pleased to tell you how the Lord delivered them. As you listen to one after another who have tried the Word of God and proved it, the Divine Spirit will lead you to believe.

Have you heard of the African who was told by the missionary that water sometimes becomes so hard that a man can walk on it? He declared that he believed a great many things the missionary had told him, but he would never believe that. When he came to England he saw the river frozen one frosty day, but he would not walk on it. He knew that it was a deep river, and he felt certain that he would be drowned if he walked on it. He could not be induced to walk on the frozen water until his friend and many others went on it. Then he was persuaded and trusted himself where others had safely walked. So, when you see others believing in the Lamb of God and notice their joy and peace, you will be gently led to believe. The experience of others is one of God's ways of helping us to faith. You have either to believe in Jesus or die. There is no hope for you but in Him.

Note the Authority You Are Commanded to Believe

A better plan is this: Note the authority upon which you are commanded to believe, and you will be greatly helped to faith. The authority is not mine, or you might well reject it. However, you are commanded to believe upon the authority of God Himself. He bids you to believe in Jesus Christ, and you must not refuse to obey your Maker.

The foreman of a certain factory had often heard the Gospel, but he was troubled with the fear that Christ might not want him. One day his employer sent him a card at the factory that read, "Come to my house immediately after work." The foreman appeared at his employer's door. The employer came out and said, somewhat roughly, "What do you want, John, troubling me at this time? Work is done; what right have you here?" "Sir," he said, "I had a card from you saying that I was to come after work." "Do you mean to say that merely because you had a card from me you came to my house and called me out after business hours?" "Well, sir," replied the foreman, "I do not understand you, but it seems to me that since you sent for me, I had a right to come." "Come in, John," said his employer. "I have another message that I want to read to you." He sat down and read these words: *"Come unto me, all ye that labour and are heavy laden, and I will give you rest"* (Matthew 11:28). "Do you think that after such a message from Christ you can be wrong in coming to Him?" The poor man saw it all at once and believed in the Lord Jesus for eternal life because he perceived that he had good warrant and authority for believing. So have you! You have good authority for coming to Christ, for the Lord Himself tells you to trust Him.

Consider What You Are to Believe

If that does not bring you faith, think over what it is that you have to believe: The Lord Jesus Christ suffered in the place and stead of sinners and is able to save all who trust Him. Why, this is the most blessed fact that men were ever told to believe. It is the most suitable, the most comforting, the most divine truth that was ever set before mortal minds. I advise you to think much about it and to search out the grace and love that it contains. Study the four Gospels, study Paul's Epistles, and then see if the message is not such a credible one that you are forced to believe it.

The Increase of Faith

Consider the Person of Jesus Christ

If that is not enough, then think about the person of Jesus Christ—think of who He is and what He did and where He is and what He is. How can you doubt Him? It is cruelty to distrust the ever truthful Jesus. He has done nothing to deserve distrust. On the contrary, it should be easy to rely on Him. Why crucify Him again by unbelief? Is this not crowning Him with thorns again and spitting on Him again? What! Is He not to be trusted? What worse insult did the soldiers pour on Him than this? They made Him a martyr, but you make Him a liar, which is far worse. Do not ask, "How can I believe?" Rather, answer another question: "How can you disbelieve?"

Submit to God

If none of these things avails, then there is something wrong with you altogether. My last word to you is this: Submit yourself to God! Prejudice or pride is at the bottom of this unbelief. May the Spirit of God take away your enmity and make you yield. You are a rebel, a proud rebel, and that is why you do not believe your God. Give up your rebellion; throw down your weapons. Yield at discretion; surrender to your King. I believe that every time a soul throws up its hands in self-despair and cries, "Lord, I yield," faith becomes easy to it before long. It is because you still quarrel with God and resolve to have your own will and your own way that you cannot believe. *"How can ye believe,"* said Christ, *"which receive honour one of another?"* (John 5:44). Proud self creates unbelief. Submit. Yield to your God, and then you will sweetly believe in your Savior. May the Holy Spirit now work secretly but effectively in you and bring you at this very moment to believe in the Lord Jesus! Amen.

Chapter 13

Regeneration and the Holy Spirit

Ye must be born again.
—John 3:7

No man can come to me, except the Father which hath sent me draw him.
—John 6:44

Y e must be born again." This word of our Lord Jesus has appeared to stand in the way of many, like the drawn sword of the cherub at the gate of Paradise (Genesis 3:24). They have despaired because this change is beyond their utmost effort. The new birth is from above, and therefore it is not in man's power. Now, it is far from my mind to deny or ever to conceal a truth in order to create a false comfort. I freely admit that the new birth is supernatural and that it cannot be done by the sinner's own self. It would be of little help to you if I were wicked enough to try to cheer you by persuading you to reject or forget what is unquestionably true.

Yet is it not remarkable that the very chapter in which our Lord makes this sweeping declaration also contains the most explicit statement as to salvation by faith? Read chapter three of John's Gospel and do not concentrate only on its earlier sentences. It is true that verse three says, *"Jesus answered and said unto him, Verily, verily, I say unto thee, Except a man be born again, he cannot see the kingdom of God."* However, verses fourteen and fifteen say, *"And as Moses lifted up the serpent in the wilderness, even so must the Son of man be lifted up: that whosoever believeth in him should not perish, but have eternal life."*

Verse eighteen repeats the same doctrine in the broadest terms: *"He that believeth on him is not condemned: but he that believeth not is condemned already, because he hath not believed in the name of the only begotten Son of God."*

It is clear that these two statements must agree, since they came from the same lips and are recorded on the same inspired page. Why should we find difficulty where there is none? One statement assures us of the necessity to salvation of something that only God can give. Another assures us that the Lord will save us when we believe in Jesus. Therefore, we may safely conclude that the Lord will give to those who believe all that is declared to be necessary for salvation. The Lord does, in fact, produce the new birth in all who believe in Jesus. Their believing is the surest evidence that they are born again.

We trust in Jesus for what we cannot do ourselves. If it were in our own power, why would we need to look to Him? It is ours to believe; it is the Lord's to create us anew. He will not believe for us; neither are we to do regenerating work for Him. It is enough for us to obey the gracious command. It is for the Lord to work the new birth in us. He who could go so far as to die on the cross for us can and will give us all things necessary for our eternal safety.

"But a saving change of heart is the work of the Holy Spirit." This statement, also, is most true, and let it be far from us to question it or to forget it. Yet the work of the Holy Spirit is secret and mysterious. It can be perceived only by its results. There are mysteries about our natural birth into which it would be an unhallowed curiosity to pry. Still more is this the case with the sacred operations of the Spirit of God. *The wind bloweth where it listeth, and thou hearest the sound thereof, but canst not tell whence it cometh, and whither it goeth: so is every one that is born of the Spirit*"

All of Grace

(John 3:8). This much, however, we do know: The mysterious work of the Holy Spirit cannot be a reason for refusing to believe in Jesus to whom that same Spirit bears witness.

If a man were told to sow a field, he could not excuse his neglect by saying that it would be useless to sow unless God caused the seed to grow. He would not be justified in neglecting tillage because the secret energy of God alone can create a harvest. No one is hindered in the ordinary pursuits of life by the fact that *"except the Lord build the house, they labour in vain that build it"* (Psalm 127:1). It is certain that no man who believes in Jesus will ever find that the Holy Spirit refuses to work in him. In fact, his believing is the proof that the Spirit is already at work in his heart.

God works in providence, but men do not, therefore, sit still. They could not move without the divine power giving them life and strength. Yet they proceed on their way without question, the power being bestowed from day to day by Him in whose hand their breath is, and by Him who guides all their ways. So is it in grace. We repent and believe, though we could do neither if the Lord did not enable us. We forsake sin and trust in Jesus. Then we perceive that the Lord has caused us *"to will and to do of his* [own] *good pleasure"* (Philippians 2:13). It is idle to pretend that there is any real difficulty in the matter.

Regeneration and the Holy Spirit

Some truths that are hard to explain in words are simple enough in actual experience. There is no discrepancy between the truth that the sinner believes and that his faith is brought about by the Holy Spirit. Only folly can lead men to puzzle themselves about plain matters while their souls are in danger. No man would refuse to enter a lifeboat because he did not know the specific gravity of bodies. Neither would a starving man decline to eat until he understood the whole process of nutrition. If you will not believe until you can understand all mysteries, you will never be saved at all. If you allow self-invented difficulties to keep you from accepting pardon through your Lord and Savior, you will perish in a condemnation that will be richly deserved. Do not commit spiritual suicide through a passion for discussing metaphysical subtleties.

Chapter 14
"My Redeemer Liveth"

I know that my redeemer liveth,
and that he shall stand
at the latter day upon the earth.
—Job 19:25

I have continually spoken to you concerning Christ crucified, who is the great hope of the guilty. Yet we will be wise to remember that our Lord has risen from the dead and lives eternally.

You are not asked to trust in a dead Jesus but in One who, though He died for our sins, has risen again *"for our justification"* (Romans 4:25). You may go to Jesus at once as to a living and present Friend. He is not a mere memory but a continually existent Person who will hear your prayers and answer them. He lives to carry on the work for which He once laid down His life. He is interceding for sinners at the right hand of the Father; for this reason, He is able to save to the uttermost those who come to God by Him (Hebrews 7:25). Come and try this living Savior if you have never done so before.

This living Jesus is also raised to an eminence of glory and power. He does not now sorrow as "a humble man before his foes," nor labor as "the carpenter's son." He is exalted *far above all principality, and power,...and every name that is named* (Ephesians 1:21). The Father has given Him *all power...in heaven and in earth* (Matthew 28:18), and He exercises this high endowment in carrying out His work of grace. Hear what Peter and the other apostles testified concerning Him before the high priest and the council:

> *The God of our fathers raised up Jesus, whom ye slew and hanged on a tree. Him hath God exalted with his right hand to be a Prince and a Saviour, for to give repentance to Israel, and forgiveness of sins.* (Acts 5:30–31)

The glory that surrounds the ascended Lord should breathe hope into every believer's breast. Jesus is no ordinary Person. He is *a saviour, and a great one* (Isaiah 19:20). He is the crowned and enthroned Redeemer of men. The sovereign prerogative of life and death is vested in Him. The Father has put all men under the mediatorial government of the Son so that He can quicken whom He will. He opens and no man shuts (Revelation 3:7). At His word, the soul that is bound by the cords of sin and condemnation can be unloosened in a moment. He stretches out the silver scepter, and whoever touches it lives.

It is a blessing for us that, as sin lives, and the flesh lives, and the devil lives, so Jesus lives. It is also a blessing that, whatever strength these may have to ruin us, Jesus has still greater power to save us.

All His exaltation and ability are on our account. He is exalted both to be and to give. He is exalted to be a Prince and a Savior so that He may give all that is needed to accomplish the salvation of all who come under His rule. Jesus *has* nothing that He will not use for a sinner's salvation, and He *is* nothing that He will not display in the abundance of His grace. He links His princedom with His saviorship, as if He would not have the one without the other. He sets forth His exaltation as designed to bring blessings to men, as if this were the flower and crown of His glory. Could anything be more suitable to raise the hopes of seeking sinners who are looking Christward?

Jesus endured great humiliation, and therefore there was room for Him to be exalted. By that humiliation He accomplished and endured all the Father's will. Therefore, He was rewarded by being raised to glory. He uses that exaltation on behalf of His people. Raise your eyes to these hills of glory, from where your help must come. Contemplate the high glories of the Prince and Savior. Is it not most hopeful for men that a Man is now on the throne of the universe? Is it not glorious that the Lord of all is the Savior of sinners? We have a Friend at court; not only this, but we have a Friend on the throne. He will use all His influence for those who entrust their affairs in His hands. One of our poets sings well:

> He ever lives to intercede
>   Before His Father's face;
> Give Him, my soul, thy cause to plead,
>   Nor doubt the Father's grace.

Come and commit your cause and your case to those once-pierced hands that are now glorified with the signet rings of royal power and honor. No case that was left with this great Advocate ever failed.

Chapter 15
Repentance Must Go with Forgiveness

Him hath God exalted with his right hand to be a Prince and a Saviour, for to give repentance to Israel, and forgiveness of sins.
—Acts 5:31

I t is clear from the above text that repentance is linked with the forgiveness of sins. In Acts 5:31, we read that Jesus is exalted to give repentance and forgiveness of sins. These two blessings come from that sacred hand that once was nailed to the tree but is now raised to glory. Repentance and forgiveness are riveted together by the eternal purpose of God. What God has joined together, let no man put asunder.

Repentance must go with remission of sins. You will understand this if you give it some thought. It cannot be that pardon of sin would be given to an impenitent sinner. This would only confirm him in his evil ways and teach him to think little of evil. If the Lord were to say, "You love sin and live in it, and you are going on from bad to worse, but all the same, I forgive you," this would proclaim a horrible license for iniquity. The foundations of social order would be removed, and moral anarchy would follow. I cannot tell what innumerable wrongs would occur if you could divide repentance and forgiveness, and could then pass by the sin while the sinner remained as fond of it as ever.

If we believe in the holiness of God, we cannot be forgiven if we continue to sin and refuse to repent of it. We will reap the consequence of our obstinacy. According to God's infinite goodness, we are promised that if we will forsake our sins, confess them, and by faith accept the grace that is provided in Christ Jesus, God *"is faithful and just to forgive us our sins, and to cleanse us from all unrighteousness"* (1 John 1:9). Yet as long as God lives, there can be no promise of mercy to those who continue in their evil ways and refuse to acknowledge their wrongdoing. Surely, no rebel can expect the King to pardon his treason while he remains in open revolt. No one can be so foolish as to imagine that the Judge of all the earth will put away our sins if we refuse to put them away ourselves.

Moreover, it must be so for the completeness of divine mercy. The mercy that could forgive the sin and yet let the sinner continue in it would be scant and superficial. It would be unequal and deformed mercy, lame in one foot and withered in one of its hands. Which do you think is the greater privilege: cleansing from the guilt of sin or deliverance from the power of sin? I will not attempt to weigh in the scales two mercies so surpassing. Neither of them could have come to us apart from the precious blood of Jesus. However, it seems to me that to be delivered from the dominion of sin and to be made holy—to be made like God—must be esteemed the greater of the two, if a comparison has to be made.

To be forgiven is an immeasurable favor. We make this one of the first notes of our psalm of praise: *"Who forgiveth all thine iniquities"* (Psalm 103:3). Yet if we could be forgiven and then could be permitted to love sin, to riot in iniquity, and to wallow in lust, what would be the use of such a forgiveness? Might it not turn out to be poisoned candy that would most effectually destroy us? To be washed and yet to lie in the dirt, to be pronounced clean and yet to have the leprosy white on one's brow, would be the worst mockery of mercy. What good is it to bring the man out of his grave if you leave him dead? Why lead him into the light if he is still blind?

We thank God that He who forgives our iniquities also heals our diseases. He who washes us from the stains of the past also uplifts us from the foul ways of the present and keeps us from falling in the future. We must joyfully accept both repentance and remission; they cannot be separated. The covenantal heritage is one and indivisible and must not be parceled out. To divide the work of grace would be like cutting a living child in half; and those who would permit this have no interest in it. (See 1 Kings 3:16–27.)

You who are seeking the Lord, would you be satisfied with one of these mercies alone? Would you be content if God would forgive your sin and then allow you to be as worldly and wicked as before? Oh, no! The quickened spirit is more afraid of sin itself than of the penal results of it. The cry of your heart is not, "Who will deliver me from punishment?" but *"O wretched man that I am! who shall deliver me from the body of this death?'* (Romans 7:24). Who will enable me to live above temptation and to become holy, even as God is holy?" Since the unity of repentance with remission agrees with gracious desire, and since it is necessary for the completeness of salvation and for holiness' sake, rest assured that it abides.

Repentance and forgiveness are joined together in the experience of all believers. There never was a person who unfeignedly repented of sin with believing repentance who was not forgiven. On the other hand, there never was a person forgiven who had not repented of his sin. I do not hesitate to say that beneath heaven there never was, there is not, and there never will be any case of sin being washed away unless, at the same time, the heart was led to repentance and faith in Christ. Hatred of sin and a sense of pardon come together into the soul and abide together while we live.

These two things act and react on each other. The man who realizes he is forgiven, therefore repents. The man who repents is also most assuredly forgiven. Remember first that Christ's forgiveness leads to repentance. As we sing, in Hart's words,

> Law and terrors do but harden
> All the while they work alone;
> But a sense of blood-bought pardon
> Soon dissolves a heart of stone.

When we are sure that we are forgiven, then we abhor iniquity. And I suppose that when faith grows into full assurance, so that we are certain beyond a doubt that the blood of Jesus has washed us whiter than snow, it is then that repentance attains its greatest height. Repentance grows as faith grows. Do not make any mistake about it. Repentance is not a thing of days and weeks, a temporary penance to be gotten over as fast as possible! No, it is the grace of a lifetime, like faith itself. God's little children repent, and so do the young men and the fathers. Repentance is the inseparable companion of faith.

All the time that we walk by faith and not by sight, the tear of repentance glistens in the eye of faith. It is not a true repentance that does not come from faith in Jesus. It is not a true faith in Jesus that is not colored with repentance. Faith and repentance, like Siamese twins, are vitally joined together. We repent in proportion to our belief in the forgiving love of Christ. We rejoice in the fullness of Jesus' absolution in proportion to our repentance of sin and our hatred of evil. You will never value pardon unless you feel repentance. You will never taste the deepest portion of repentance until you know that you are pardoned. It may seem like a strange thing, and so it is. The bitterness of repentance and the sweetness of pardon blend in the flavor of every gracious life and make up an incomparable happiness.

These two covenantal gifts are the mutual assurance of each other. If I know that I repent, I know that I am forgiven. How am I to know that I am forgiven except that I also know that I have turned from my former sinful course? To be a believer is to be a penitent. Faith and repentance are but two spokes in the same wheel, two handles of the same plow. Repentance has been well described as a heart broken for sin and from sin. It may equally well be spoken of as turning and returning. It is a change of mind of the most thorough and radical sort. It is attended with sorrow for the past and a resolve of amendment in the future.

> Repentance is to leave
> The sins we loved before;
> And show that we in earnest grieve,
> By doing so no more.

Now, when that is the case, we may be certain that we are forgiven, for the Lord never caused a heart to be broken for sin and broken from sin without pardoning it. If, on the other hand, we are enjoying pardon through the blood of Jesus and are justified by faith and have peace with God through Jesus Christ our Lord (Romans 5:1), we know that our repentance and faith are of the right sort.

Do not regard your repentance as the cause of your remission, but as the companion of it. Do not expect to be able to repent until you are able to see the grace of our Lord Jesus and His readiness to blot out your sin. Keep these blessed things in their places, and view them in their relation to each other. They are the Jachin and Boaz of a saving experience. I mean that they are comparable to Solomon's two great pillars that stood in the forefront of the house of the Lord and formed a majestic entrance to the holy place. (See 1 Kings 7:21.) No man comes to God properly unless he passes between the pillars of repentance and remission. The rainbow of covenantal grace has been displayed upon your heart in all its beauty when the teardrops of repentance have been shone upon by the light of full forgiveness. Repentance of sin and faith in divine pardon are the intertwining threads of the fabric of real conversion. By these characteristics, you will know a true Israelite.

To come back to the Scripture on which we are meditating, both forgiveness and repentance flow from the same source and are given by the same Savior. The Lord Jesus in His glory bestows both on the same people. You can find neither the remission nor the repentance elsewhere. Jesus has both ready, and He is prepared to bestow them now and to bestow them most freely on all who will accept them at His hands. Never forget that Jesus gives all that is needed for our salvation. It is very important that all seekers after mercy remember this fact. Faith is as much the gift of God as is the Savior upon whom that faith relies. Repentance of sin is as truly the work of grace as the making of an atonement by which sin is blotted out. Salvation, from first to last, is of grace alone.

Do not misunderstand me. It is not the Holy Spirit who repents. He has never done anything for which He should repent. If He could repent, it would not help us. We ourselves must repent of our own sin, or we are not saved from its power. It is also not the Lord Jesus Christ who repents. What should He repent of? We ourselves repent with the full consent of every faculty of our minds. The will, the affections, and the emotions all work together most heartily in the blessed act of repentance for sin. And yet, behind all that is our personal act, there is a secret holy influence that melts the heart, gives contrition, and produces a complete change.

The Spirit of God enlightens us to see what sin is and thus makes it loathsome in our eyes. The Spirit of God also turns us toward holiness. He makes us greatly appreciate, love, and desire it, and thus gives us the impetus by which we are led onward from stage to stage of sanctification. The Spirit of God works in us to will and to do according to God's good pleasure (Philippians 2:13). To that Good Spirit let us submit ourselves at once so that He may lead us to Jesus, who will freely give us the double benediction of repentance and remission, *"according to the riches of his grace"* (Ephesians 1:7). *"By grace are ye saved"* (Ephesians 2:8).

Chapter 16

How Repentance Is Given

*Him hath God exalted with his right hand
to be a Prince and a Saviour, for to give
repentance to Israel,
and forgiveness of sins.*
—Acts 5:31

Return to the grand text, *"Him hath God exalted with his right hand to be a Prince and a Saviour, for to give repentance to Israel, and forgiveness of sins."* Our Lord Jesus Christ has gone up so that grace may come down. His glory is employed to give greater currency to His grace. The Lord has not taken a step upward except with the design of bearing believing sinners upward with Him. He is exalted to give repentance, and we will see this if we remember a few great truths.

Christ Has Made Repentance Possible, Available, and Acceptable

The work that our Lord Jesus has done has made repentance possible, available, and acceptable. The Old Testament makes no mention of repentance, but says plainly, *"The soul that sinneth, it shall die"* (Ezekiel 18:20). If the Lord Jesus had not died and risen again and gone to the Father, what would our repenting be worth? We might feel remorse with its horrors, but never repentance with its hopes. Repentance, as a natural feeling, is a common duty deserving no great praise. Indeed, it is so generally mingled with a selfish fear of punishment that the kindest estimate makes little of it. Had Jesus not interposed and accomplished a wealth of merit, our tears of repentance would have been so much water spilled on the ground. Jesus is exalted on high so that through the virtue of His intercession, repentance may have a place before God. In this respect, He gives us repentance because He puts repentance into a position of acceptance that otherwise it could never have occupied.

How Repentance Is Given

The Holy Spirit Renews Our Nature

When Jesus was exalted on high, the Spirit of God was poured out to work all needful graces in us. The Holy Spirit creates repentance in us by supernaturally renewing our nature and taking the heart of stone out of our flesh. Oh, do not strain those eyes of yours to make impossible tears! Repentance does not come from an unwilling nature, but from free and sovereign grace. Do not go to your room to punish yourself, as if to bring from a heart of stone feelings that are not there. Rather, go to Calvary and see how Jesus died. Look upward to the hills from where your help comes. The Holy Spirit has come with the purpose that He may overshadow men's spirits and breed repentance within them, even as He once brooded over chaos and brought forth order. (See Genesis 1.) Breathe your prayer to Him: "Blessed Spirit, dwell with me. Make me tender and lowly of heart that I may hate sin and unfeignedly repent of it." He will hear your cry and answer you.

The Works of Nature and Providence Are Consecrated for Our Salvation

Remember, too, that, when our Lord Jesus was exalted, He gave us repentance not only by sending forth the Holy Spirit, but also by consecrating all the works of nature and of providence to the great ends of our salvation. In this way, any one of them may call us to repentance, whether it crow like Peter's rooster (see Matthew 26:33–35, 47–58, 69–74) or shake the prison like the jailer's earthquake (Acts 16:23–34). From the right hand of God, our Lord Jesus rules all things here below and makes them work together for the salvation of His redeemed. He uses both bitter and sweet things, trials and joys, so that He may produce in sinners a better mind toward their God. Be thankful for the providence that has made you poor or sick or sad. By all this Jesus works the life of your spirit and turns you to Himself. The Lord's mercy often rides to the door of our hearts on the black horse of affliction. Jesus uses the whole range of our experience to wean us from earth and woo us to heaven. Christ is exalted to the throne of heaven and earth in order that, by all the processes of His providence, He may subdue hard hearts to the gracious softening of repentance.

Christ Has Abundant Ways of Bringing About Repentance

Besides, He is at work this hour by all His whispers in the conscience, by His inspired Book, by those of us who speak out of that Book, and by praying friends and earnest hearts. He can send a word to you that will strike your rocky heart as with the rod of Moses and cause streams of repentance to flow forth. He can bring to your mind some heartbreaking text out of Holy Scripture that will conquer you immediately. He can mysteriously soften you and cause a holy frame of mind to steal over you when you least look for it. Be sure of this: He who is gone into His glory, raised into all the splendor and majesty of God, has abundant ways of working repentance in those to whom He grants forgiveness. Even now, He is waiting to give repentance to you. Ask Him for it at once.

Repentance Is Given to the Most Unlikely People

Observe with great comfort that the Lord Jesus Christ gives this repentance to the most unlikely people in the world. He is exalted *"to give repentance to Israel."* Israel! In the days when the apostles spoke this, Israel was the nation that had most grossly sinned against light and love by daring to say, *"His blood be on us, and on our children"* (Matthew 27:25). Yet Jesus is exalted to give *them* repentance! What a marvel of grace! If you have been brought up in the brightest of Christian light and yet have rejected it, there is still hope. If you have sinned against conscience and against the Holy Spirit and against the love of Jesus, there is still room for repentance. Though you may be as hard as unbelieving Israel of old, softening may yet come to you, since Jesus is exalted and clothed with boundless power. For those who went the furthest in iniquity and sinned with special aggravation, the Lord Jesus is exalted to give to them *"repentance...and forgiveness of sins."* I am happy to have so full a Gospel to proclaim! Happy are you to be allowed to read it!

The hearts of the children of Israel had grown as hard as stone. Luther used to think it impossible to convert a Jew. We are far from agreeing with him. Yet we must admit that the children of Israel have been exceedingly obstinate in their rejection of the Savior during these many centuries. Truly did the Lord say, *"Israel would* [have] *none of me"* (Psalm 81:11). *"He came unto his own, and his own received him not"* (John 1:11). However, on behalf of Israel, our Lord Jesus is exalted for the giving of repentance and remission. You are probably a Gentile, but yet you may have a very stubborn heart that has stood against the Lord Jesus for many years. Even so, our Lord can work repentance in you. It may be that you will feel compelled to write as William Hone did when he yielded to divine love. He was the author of some entertaining volumes called the *Everyday Book,* but he was once an out-and-out atheist. When subdued by sovereign grace, he wrote,

> The proudest heart that ever beat
> Hath been subdued in me;

How Repentance Is Given

The wildest will that ever rose
To scorn Thy cause and aid Thy foes
    Is quell'd my Lord, by Thee.
Thy will, and not my will be done,
    My heart be ever Thine;
Confessing Thee the mighty Word,
My Savior Christ, my God, my Lord,
    Thy cross shall be my sign.

The Lord can give repentance to the most unlikely—turning lions into lambs, and ravens into doves. Let us look to Him so that this great change may take place in us.

Meditate on Christ's Sacrificial Death

Assuredly, the contemplation of the death of Christ is one of the surest and speediest methods of gaining repentance. Do not sit down and try to pump up repentance from the dry well of a corrupt nature. It is contrary to the laws of your mind to suppose that you can force your soul into that gracious state. Take your heart in prayer to Him who understands it and say, "Lord, cleanse it. Lord, renew it. Lord, work repentance in it." The more you try to produce penitent emotions in yourself, the more you will be disappointed. However, if you believingly think of Jesus dying for you, repentance will burst forth.

All of Grace

Meditate on the Lord's shedding His heart's blood out of love for you. Set before your mind's eye the agony and bloody sweat, the cross and passion. As you do this, He who was the Bearer of all this grief will look at you. With that look, He will do for you what He did for Peter, so that you also will go out and weep bitterly (Matthew 26:75). He who died for you can, by His gracious Spirit, make you die to sin. He who has gone into glory on your behalf can draw your soul after Him, away from evil and toward holiness.

I will be content if I leave this one thought with you: Do not look beneath the ice to find fire, nor hope in your own natural heart to find repentance. Look to the Living One for life. Look to Jesus for all you need between the gate of hell and the gate of heaven. Never seek elsewhere for any part of what Jesus loves to bestow, but remember that Christ is all.

Chapter 17
The Fear of Final Falling

*Now unto him that is able to keep you
from falling, and to present you
faultless before the presence of his
glory with exceeding joy.*
—Jude 24

A dark fear haunts the minds of many who are coming to Christ. They are afraid that they will not persevere to the end. I have heard the seeker say, "If I were to cast my soul on Jesus, perhaps I would, after all, draw back into perdition. I have had good feelings before now, and they have died away. My goodness has been as the morning cloud and as the early dew. It has come suddenly, lasted for a season, promised much, and then vanished away."

All of Grace

I believe that this fear is often the father of the fact, and that some who have been afraid to trust Christ for all time and eternity have failed because they had a temporary faith that never went far enough to save them. They set out trusting Jesus in a measure, yet looking to themselves for continuance and perseverance in the heavenward way. So they set out faultily and, as a natural consequence, turned back before long. If we trust in ourselves for our holding on, we will not hold on. Even though we rest in Jesus for a part of our salvation, we will fail if we trust in self for anything. No chain is stronger than its weakest link. If Jesus is our hope for everything except one thing, we will utterly fail, because in that one point we will come to nothing.

Look to Christ as Your Strength from Beginning to End

I have no doubt whatever that a mistaken idea about the perseverance of the saints has prevented the perseverance of many who ran well. What hindered them so that they did not continue to run? They trusted in themselves for that running, and so they stopped short. Beware of mixing even a little of self with the mortar with which you build, or you will make it untempered mortar. The stones will not hold together. If you look to Christ for your beginning, beware of looking to yourself for your ending. He is Alpha. See to it that you make Him Omega, also. If you begin in the Spirit, you must not hope to be made perfect by the flesh (Galatians 3:3). Begin as you intend to go on, and go on as you began. Let the Lord be all in all to you. Oh, that God the Holy Spirit may give us a very clear idea of where the strength must come from by which we will be preserved until the Day of our Lord's appearing!

Here is what Paul said on this subject when he was writing to the Corinthians:

> *Our Lord Jesus Christ...shall also confirm you unto the end, that ye may be blameless in the day of our Lord Jesus Christ. God is faithful, by whom ye were called unto the fellowship of his Son Jesus Christ our Lord.*　　　(1 Corinthians 1:7–9)

This language silently admits a great need by telling us how it is provided for. Wherever the Lord makes a provision, we are quite sure that there was a need for it. No superfluities clutter the covenant of grace. Golden shields that hung in Solomon's courts were never used, but there are none such in the armory of God. What God has provided, we will surely need. Between this hour and the consummation of all things, every promise of God and every provision of the covenant of grace will be brought into requisition. The urgent need of the believing soul is confirmation, continuance, final perseverance, preservation to the end. This is the great necessity of the most advanced believers, for Paul was writing to saints at Corinth who were men of a high order, of whom he could say, *"I thank my God always on your behalf, for the grace of God which is given you by Jesus Christ"* (1 Corinthians 1:4).

Such men are the very people who most assuredly feel that they have daily need of a new grace if they are to hold on and hold out and become conquerors at the last. If you were not saints, you would have no grace, and you would feel no need of more grace. However, because you are men of God, you feel the daily demands of the spiritual life. The marble statue requires no food, but the living man hungers and thirsts. He rejoices that his bread and his water are guaranteed for him, or else he would certainly faint by the way. The believer's personal needs make it inevitable that he should draw daily from the great Source of all supplies. What could he do if he could not resort to his God?

This is true of the most gifted of the saints, as it was of those men at Corinth who were *"enriched...in all utterance, and in all knowledge"* (v. 5). They needed to be confirmed to the end (v. 8) or else their gifts and achievements would have proved to be their ruin. If we had the tongues of men and of angels, yet we did not receive fresh grace, where would we be? If we had all experience until we were fathers in the church—if we had been taught by God so as to understand all mysteries—even so, we could not live a single day without the divine life flowing into us from our covenant Head. How could we hope to hold on for a single hour, to say nothing of a lifetime, unless the Lord held onto us? He who began the good work in us must *"perform it until the day of Jesus Christ"* (Philippians 1:6), or it will prove to be a painful failure.

Why We Need Christ to Uphold Us

Fickleness of Heart

The great necessity arises very much from our own selves. In some there is a painful fear that they will not persevere in grace because they know their own fickleness. Certain people are constitutionally unstable. Some men are by nature conservative, not to mention obstinate. Yet others are just as naturally variable and volatile. Like butterflies, they flit from flower to flower until they visit all the beauties of the garden and settle upon none of them. They are never in one place long enough to do any good, not in their business nor in their intellectual pursuits. Such people may well be afraid that ten, twenty, thirty, forty, perhaps fifty years of continuous Christian watchfulness will be too much for them. We see men joining one church and then another until they have tried them all. They do everything in phases and nothing in a long-lasting way. Such people need to pray twice as much that they may be divinely confirmed and may be made not only steadfast but also unmovable (1 Corinthians 15:58). Otherwise, they will not be found *"always abounding in the work of the Lord"* (v. 58).

All of us, even if we have no natural inclination to fickleness, must feel our own weakness if we are really quickened by God. Is there not enough in any one single day to make you stumble? You who desire to walk in perfect holiness and you who have set before yourself a high standard of what a Christian should be, do you not find that before the breakfast things are cleared away from the table you have displayed enough sin to make you ashamed of yourselves? If we were to shut ourselves up in the lone cell of a hermit, temptation would follow us. As long as we cannot escape from ourselves, we cannot escape from incitements to sin. There is within our hearts that which should make us watchful and humble before God. If He does not confirm us, we are so weak that we will stumble and fall—not overturned by an enemy but by our own carelessness. Lord, be our strength. We are weakness itself.

Weariness with Life

Besides that, there is the weariness that comes with a long life. When we begin our Christian profession, we mount up with wings as eagles. Further on, we run without weariness. Yet in our best and truest days, we walk without fainting. (See Isaiah 40:31.) Our pace seems slower, but it is more serviceable and better sustained. I pray God that the energy of our youth may continue with us as long as it is the energy of the Spirit and not the mere energy of proud flesh. He who has been on the road to heaven for a long time finds that there was a good reason why it was promised that his shoes would be iron and brass (Deuteronomy 33:25): The road is rough. He has discovered, as did John Bunyan's famous Pilgrim, that there are Hills of Difficulty and Valleys of Humiliation. He has learned that there is a Valley of the Shadow of Death and, worse still, a Vanity Fair. All these are to be experienced. If there are Delectable Mountains (and, thank God, there are), there are also castles of Giant Despair, the inside of which pilgrims have too often seen. Considering all things, those who hold out to the end in the way of holiness will be *"men wondered at"* (Zechariah 3:8).

"O world of wonders, I can say no less." The days of a Christian's life are like so many Koh-i-noors* of mercy threaded on the golden string of divine faithfulness. In heaven, we will tell angels

---

* The Koh-i-noor is an Indian diamond, weighing 106 carats, that was acquired by the British. It became the central stone in the crown worn by Elizabeth, the Queen Mother, at the coronation of her husband, George VI, in 1937.

and principalities and powers the unsearchable riches of Christ that were spent on us and enjoyed by us while we were here below. We have been kept alive on the brink of death. Our spiritual lives have been as a flame burning on in the midst of the sea. They have been as a stone that has remained suspended in the air. It will amaze the universe to see us enter the pearly gates blameless in the Day of our Lord Jesus Christ. We should be full of grateful wonder if we are kept by Him for an hour, and I trust we are.

The Wilderness of the World

If this were all, there would be enough cause for anxiety, but there is far more. We have to think of what a place we live in. The world is a howling wilderness to many of God's people. Some of us are greatly indulged in the providence of God, but others have a stern fight of it. We begin our day with prayer, and many of us very often hear the voice of holy song in our houses. Yet many good people have scarcely risen from their knees in the morning before they are greeted with blasphemy. They go out to work and all day long are distressed, like righteous Lot in Sodom, over having to listen to filthy conversation. Can you even walk the open streets without your ears being afflicted with foul language? The world is no friend to grace. The best we can do with this world is to get through it with Jesus as close to us as possible. We live in an enemy's country. A "robber" lurks in every bush. We need to travel everywhere with a "drawn sword" in our hand (Ephesians 6:17), or at least with that weapon that is called *"all prayer"* (v. 18) at our side. We have to fight for every inch of our way. Make no mistake about this, or you will be rudely shaken out of your fond delusion. O God, help us and confirm us to the end, or where will we be?

He Will Keep You from Falling

True Christianity is supernatural at its beginning, supernatural in its continuance, and supernatural in its close. It is the work of God from first to last. There is great need for the hand of the Lord to be stretched out still. You are feeling that need now, and I am glad that you feel it. Now you will look for your own preservation to the Lord, who alone is able to keep us from falling and glorify us with His Son.

Chapter 18
Confirmation

Christ...shall also confirm you unto the end,
that ye may be blameless in the day
of our Lord Jesus Christ.
—1 Corinthians 1:7–8

Notice the security that Paul confidently expected for all the saints. He said, "*Christ...shall also confirm you unto the end, that ye may be blameless in the day of our Lord Jesus Christ.*" This is the kind of confirmation that is to be desired above all things. It supposes that the people are right, and it proposes to confirm them in the right. It would be an awful thing to confirm a man in ways of sin and error. Think of a confirmed drunkard or a confirmed thief or a confirmed liar. It would be a deplorable thing for a man to be confirmed in unbelief and ungodliness. Divine confirmation can be enjoyed only by those to whom the grace of God

All of Grace

has already been manifested. It is the work of the Holy Spirit.

He who gives faith strengthens and establishes it. He who kindles love in us preserves it and increases its flame. What He causes us to know by His first teaching, the Holy Spirit causes us to know with greater clearness and certainty by still further instruction. Holy acts are confirmed until they become habits, and holy feelings are confirmed until they become abiding conditions. Experience and practice confirm our beliefs and our resolutions. Both our joys and our sorrows, our successes and our failures, are sanctified to the same end, even as the tree is helped to take root both by the soft showers and the rough winds. The mind is instructed, and in its growing knowledge it gathers reasons for persevering in the good way. The heart is comforted, and so it is made to cling more closely to the consoling truth. The grip grows tighter, the tread grows firmer, and the man himself becomes more solid and substantial.

This is not merely natural growth, but is as distinct a work of the Spirit as is conversion. The Lord will surely give it to those who are relying on Him for eternal life. By His inward working, He will deliver us from being *"unstable as water"* (Genesis 49:4) and cause us to be *"rooted and grounded"* (Ephesians 3:17). This building us up into Christ Jesus and causing us to abide in Him is a part of the method by which He saves us. You may look for it daily, and you will not be disappointed. He whom you trust will make you to be as a tree planted by the river of water, so preserved that even your leaf will not wither (Psalm 1:3).

What strength a confirmed Christian is to a church! He is a comfort to the sorrowful and a help to the weak. Would you not like to be such? Confirmed believers are pillars in the house of our God (Revelation 3:12). They are not carried away by *"every wind of doctrine"* (Ephesians 4:14), nor overthrown by sudden temptation. They are a great inspiration to others and act as anchors in times of church trouble. You who are beginning the holy life hardly dare to hope that you will become like them. Yet you need not fear; the Good Lord will work in you as well as in them. One of these days, you who are now a "babe" in Christ will be a "father" in the church. Hope for this great thing. Hope for it as a gift of grace and not as the wages of work or as the product of your own energy.

Confirmed to the End

The inspired apostle Paul spoke of these people as those who would be confirmed *"unto the end."* He expected the grace of God to preserve them personally to the end of their lives, or until the Lord Jesus returned. Indeed, he expected that the whole church of God, in every place and in all time, would be kept to the end of the dispensation, until the Lord Jesus as the Bridegroom would come to celebrate the Wedding Feast with His perfected bride. All who are in Christ will be confirmed in Him until that illustrious day. Has He not said, *"Because I live, ye shall live also"* (John 14:19)? He also said, *"I give unto them* [My sheep] *eternal life; and they shall never perish, neither shall any man pluck them out of my hand"* (John 10:28). *"He which hath begun a good work in you will perform it until the day of Jesus Christ"* (Philippians 1:6).

The work of grace in the soul is not a superficial reformation. The life implanted as the new birth comes from a living and incorruptible seed *"which liveth and abideth for ever"* (1 Peter 1:23). And the promises of God made to believers are not of a transient character. They involve, for their fulfillment, the believer's "holding on his way" until he comes to endless glory. We are *"kept by the power of God through faith unto salvation"* (v. 5). *"The righteous also shall hold on his way"* (Job 17:9). Not as the result of our own merit or strength, but as a gift of free and undeserved favor, those who believe are *"preserved in Jesus Christ"* (Jude 1). Jesus will lose none of the sheep of His fold. No member of His body will wither; no gem of His treasure will be missing in the day when He makes up His jewels (Malachi 3:17).

Confirmation

The salvation that is received by faith is not a thing of months and years, for our Lord Jesus has *"obtained eternal redemption for us"* (Hebrews 9:12). What is eternal cannot come to an end.

Confirmed Blameless

Paul also declared his expectation that the Corinthian saints would be confirmed *"blameless"* to the end. This blamelessness is a precious part of our keeping. To be kept holy is better than merely to be kept safe. It is a dreadful thing when you see religious people blundering out of one dishonor into another. They have not believed in the power of our Lord to make them blameless. The lives of some professing Christians are a series of stumbles. They are never quite down, yet they are seldom on their feet. This is not a fit thing for a believer. He is invited to walk with God. By faith, he can attain steady perseverance in holiness, and he should do so. The Lord is able not only to save us from hell, but also to keep us from falling (Jude 24). We need not yield to temptation. Is it not written, *"Sin shall not have dominion over you"* (Romans 6:14)? The Lord is able to keep the feet of His saints, and He will do it if we will trust Him to do so. We need not defile our garments; we may by His grace keep them *"unspotted from the world"* (James 1:27). We are bound to do this, for without holiness *"no man shall see the Lord"* (Hebrews 12:14).

All of Grace

The apostle prophesied for these believers what he would have us seek after—that we may be preserved *"blameless in the day of our Lord Jesus Christ."* The *Revised Version* has *"unreproveable"* instead of *"blameless."* Possibly a better rendering would be "unimpeachable." God grant that in that last great Day we may stand free from all charge, that no one in the whole universe may dare to challenge our claim to be the redeemed of the Lord. We have sins and infirmities to mourn over, but these are not the kind of faults that would prove us to be out of Christ. We will be clear of hypocrisy, deceit, hatred, and delight in sin, for these things would be fatal charges.

Despite our failings, the Holy Spirit can work in us a character spotless before men so that, like Daniel, we will not provide an occasion for accusing tongues, except in the matter of our faith. Multitudes of godly men and women have exhibited lives so transparent, so consistent throughout, that no one could say anything against them. The Lord will be able to say of many a believer, as he did of Job when Satan stood before Him, *"Hast thou considered my servant..., a perfect and an upright man, one that feareth God, and escheweth evil?"* (Job 1:8). This is what you must look for at the Lord's hands. This is the triumph of the saints—to continue to follow the Lamb wherever He goes, maintaining our integrity as before the living God. May we never turn aside into *"crooked ways"* (Psalm 125:5) and give the adversary cause to blaspheme. (See 2 Samuel 12:14.) Of the true believer it is written, *"He...keepeth himself, and that wicked one toucheth him not"* (1 John 5:18). May it be so written concerning us!

If you are just beginning in the divine life, the Lord can give you an irreproachable character. Even though, in your past life, you may have gone far into sin, the Lord can altogether deliver you from the power of former habits and make you an example of virtue. Not only can He make you moral, but He can also make you abhor every false way and follow after all that is saintly. Do not doubt it. The chief of sinners need not be a step behind the purest of the saints. Believe this, and according to your faith it will be unto you.

Oh, what a joy it will be to be found blameless in the Day of Judgment! We do not sing amiss when we join in this charming hymn:

Bold shall I stand in that great day,
    For who aught to my charge shall lay?
While by my Lord absolved I am,
    From sin's tremendous curse and blame.
                    —Count Zinzendorf

What bliss it will be to enjoy that dauntless courage when heaven and earth will flee from the face of the Judge of all! This bliss will be the portion of everyone who looks only to the grace of God in Christ Jesus and in that sacred power wages continual war with all sin.

Chapter 19
Why Saints Persevere

God is faithful, by whom ye were called unto the fellowship of his Son Jesus Christ.
—1 Corinthians 1:9

We have already seen that the hope that filled Paul's heart concerning the Corinthian saints was a great comfort to those who feared their future. Yet why was it that he believed that the saints would be confirmed unto the end?

I want you to notice that he gave his reasons. Here they are: *"God is faithful, by whom ye were called unto the fellowship of his Son Jesus Christ."*

"God Is Faithful"

The apostle did not say, "You are faithful." The faithfulness of man is very unreliable; it is mere vanity. He did not say, "You have faithful ministers to lead and guide you, and therefore I trust you will be safe." Oh, no! If we are kept by men, we will be badly kept. He said, *"God is faithful."* If we are found faithful, it will be because God is faithful. The whole burden of our salvation must rest on the faithfulness of our covenant God. On this glorious attribute of God the matter hinges. We are as variable as the wind, as frail as a spider's web, as *"weak as water"* (Ezek 7:17; 21:7). No dependence can be placed on our natural qualities or our spiritual attainments, but God remains faithful.

He is faithful in His love; He knows no *"variableness, neither shadow of turning"* (James 1:17). He is faithful to His purpose; He does not begin a work and then leave it undone. He is faithful to His relationships. As a Father He will not renounce His children; as a Friend He will not deny His people; as a Creator He will not forsake the work of His own hands. He is faithful to His promises and will never allow one of them to fail for a single believer. He is faithful to His covenant, which He has made with us in Christ Jesus and ratified with the blood of His sacrifice. He is faithful to His Son and will not allow His precious blood to be spilled in vain. He is faithful to His people, to whom He has promised eternal life and from whom He will not turn away.

This faithfulness of God is the foundation and cornerstone of our hope of final perseverance.

Why Saints Persevere

The saints will persevere in holiness because God perseveres in grace. He perseveres to bless, and therefore believers persevere in being blessed. He continues to keep His people, and therefore they continue to keep His commandments. This is good solid ground to rest on. It is delightfully consistent with the title of this book, *All of Grace*. Thus, it is free favor and infinite mercy that ring in the dawn of salvation; and the same sweet bells sound melodiously through the whole day of grace.

Reasons the Saints Will Be Confirmed unto the End

What God Has Already Done

You see that the only reasons for hoping that we will be confirmed to the end and be found blameless at the last are found in our God. Yet, in Him, these reasons are exceedingly abundant.

They lie first in what God has done. He has gone so far in blessing us that it is not possible for Him to turn back. Paul reminded us that He has called us *"unto the fellowship of his Son Jesus Christ."* Has He called us? Then the call cannot be reversed, *"for the gifts and calling of God are without repentance"* (Romans 11:29). The Lord never turns from the effectual call of His grace. *"Whom he called, them he also justified: and whom he justified, them he also glorified"* (Romans 8:30). This is the invariable rule of the divine procedure.

All of Grace

There is a common call of which it is said, *"Many are called, but few are chosen"* (Matthew 22:14). Yet what we are now thinking of is another kind of call that means special love and necessitates the possession of that to which we are called. In such a case, it is with the called one even as with Abraham's seed, of whom the Lord said, *"Thou whom I have taken from the ends of the earth, and called thee from the chief men thereof, and said unto thee, Thou art my servant; I have chosen thee, and not cast thee away"* (Isaiah 41:9).

Our Fellowship with Jesus Christ

In what the Lord has done, we see strong reasons for our preservation and future glory because the Lord has called us into *"the fellowship of his Son Jesus Christ."* This means into partnership with Jesus Christ, and I want you to carefully consider what this signifies. If you are indeed called by divine grace, you have come into fellowship with the Lord Jesus Christ. You are joint-owner with Him in all things (Romans 8:17). Henceforth, you are one with Him in the sight of the Most High. The Lord Jesus bore your sins *"in his own body on the tree"* (1 Peter 2:24), *"being made a curse for* [you]*"* (Galatians 3:13); at the same time, He has become your righteousness, so that you are justified in Him. You are Christ's and Christ is yours.

As Adam stood for his descendants, so Jesus stands for all who are in Him. As husband and wife are one, so is Jesus one with all those who are united to Him by faith—they are one by a conjugal union that can never be broken. More than this, believers are members of the body of Christ, and so they are one with Him by a loving, living, lasting union. God has called us into this union, this fellowship, this partnership. By this very calling, He has given us the token and pledge of our being confirmed to the end. If we were considered apart from Christ, we would be poor, perishable units, soon dissolved and carried away to destruction. However, because we are one with Jesus, we are made partakers of His nature and are endowed with His immortal life. Our destiny is linked with that of our Lord, and until *He* can be destroyed, it is not possible that we would perish.

Deeply contemplate this partnership with the Son of God unto which you have been called, for all your hope lies there. You can never be poor while Jesus is rich, because you are as in one firm with Him. Want can never assail you, since you are joint-proprietor with Him who is Possessor of heaven and earth. You can never fail. Though one of the partners in the firm is as poor as a church mouse, an utter bankrupt who could not pay even a small amount of his heavy debts, yet the other Partner is inconceivably, inexhaustibly rich. In such a partnership, you are raised above the depression of the times, the changes of the future, and the shock of the end of all things. The Lord has called you into *"the fellowship of his Son Jesus Christ,"* and by that act and deed He has put you into the place of infallible safeguard.

If you are indeed a believer, you are one with Jesus, and therefore you are secure. Do you not see that it must be so? You must be confirmed to the end until the Day of His appearing, if you have indeed been made one with Jesus by the irrevocable act of God. Christ and the believing sinner are in the same boat. Unless Jesus sinks, the believer will never drown. Jesus has taken His redeemed into such connection with Himself that He must first be struck down, overcome, and dishonored before the least of His purchased ones can be injured. His name is at the head of the firm, and because He cannot be dishonored, we are secure against all dread of failure.

Linked with Jesus, Leaning on Jesus

So, then, with the utmost confidence, let us go forward into the unknown future, linked eternally with Jesus. If the men of the world cry, *"Who is this that cometh up from the wilderness, leaning upon her beloved?"* (Song of Solomon 8:5), we will joyfully confess that we do lean on Jesus and that we intend to lean on Him more and more. Our faithful God is an ever flowing well of delight, and our fellowship with the Son of

Why Saints Persevere

God is a full river of joy. Knowing these glorious things, we cannot be discouraged. Rather, we cry with the apostle, *"Who shall separate us from the love of...God, which is in Christ Jesus our Lord?"* (Romans 8:35, 39).

Chapter 20
Conclusion

*As I live, saith the Lord GOD, I have no pleasure
in the death of the wicked; but that the wicked
turn from his way and live: turn ye, turn ye from
your evil ways; for why will ye die?*
—Ezekiel 33:11

I f you have not followed me step-by-step as you have read these pages, I am truly sorry. Book reading is of little value unless the truths that pass before the mind are grasped, appropriated, and carried out in a practical way. It is as if one saw plenty of food in a store and yet remained hungry for lack of actually eating some. It is all in vain that you and I have met unless you have actually laid hold of Christ Jesus my Lord. On my part, there was a distinct desire to benefit you, and I have done my best to that end. It pains me if I have not been able to do you good, for I have longed to win that privilege.

167

All of Grace

I was thinking of you when I wrote this page, and I laid down my pen and solemnly bowed in prayer for everyone who would read it.

Why Should You Refuse?

It is my firm conviction that great numbers of readers will get a blessing, even if you refuse to be among them. Yet why should you refuse? If you do not desire the choice blessing that I would have brought to you, at least do me the justice to admit that the blame of your final doom will not lie at my door. When we meet before the Great White Throne, you will not be able to charge me with having idly used the attention that you were pleased to give me while you were reading my book. God knows I wrote each line for your eternal good. I now in spirit take you by the hand with a firm grip. Do you feel my brotherly grasp? The tears are in my eyes as I look at you and say, "Why will you die? Will you not give your soul a thought? Will you perish through sheer carelessness? Oh, do not do so, but weigh these solemn matters and make sure of eternity! Do not refuse Jesus, His love, His blood, His salvation. Why should you do so? Can you do it? I beseech you, do not turn away from your Redeemer! "

Let Jesus Be Your All in All

If, on the other hand, my prayers are heard and you have been led to trust the Lord Jesus and receive from Him salvation by grace, then keep this doctrine and this way of living. Let Jesus be your all in all, and let free grace be the one line in which you live and move. There is no life like that of one who lives in the favor of God. To receive all as a free gift preserves the mind from self-righteous pride and from self-accusing despair. It makes the heart grow warm with grateful love. It thus creates a feeling in the soul that is infinitely more acceptable to God than anything that can possibly come from slavish fear.

Those who hope to be saved by trying to do their best know nothing of that glowing fervor, that hallowed warmth, that devout joy in God that come with salvation freely given according to the grace of God. The slavish spirit of self-salvation is no match for the joyous spirit of adoption. There is more real virtue in the least emotion of faith than in all the efforts of legalistic bondslaves or all the weary machinery of devotees who would climb to heaven by means of ceremonies. Faith is spiritual, and God, who is a Spirit, delights in it for that reason. Years of saying prayers, and church or chapel going, and ceremonies and performances, may be only an abomination in the sight of Jehovah. Yet a glance from the eye of true faith is spiritual and is therefore dear to Him. *"The Father seeketh such to worship him"* (John 4:23). Look first to the inner man and to the spiritual; the rest will then follow in due course.

All of Grace

If you are saved, be on the watch for the souls of others. Your own heart will not prosper unless it is filled with intense concern to bless your fellowmen. The life of your soul lies in faith; its health lies in love. He who does not long to lead others to Jesus has never been under the influence of love himself. Get busy doing the work of the Lord, the work of love. Begin at home. Visit your neighbors next. Enlighten the town or the street where you live. Scatter the Word of the Lord wherever your hand can reach.

Believe in Jesus Now

Meet me in heaven! Do not go down to hell. There is no coming back again from that abode of misery. Why do you wish to enter the way of death when heaven's gate is open before you? Do not refuse the free pardon, the full salvation, that Jesus grants to all who trust Him. Do not hesitate and delay. You have had enough of resolving; come to action. Believe in Jesus now with full and immediate decision. Take with you words and come to your Lord this day, even this day. Remember, O soul, it may be now or never with you. Let it be now; it would be horrible if it were never.

Again I charge you, *meet me in heaven.*

About the Author

C harles Haddon Spurgeon was born on June 19, 1834, at Kelvedon, Essex, England, the firstborn of eight surviving children. His parents were committed Christians, and his father was a preacher. Spurgeon was converted in 1850 at the age of fifteen. He began to help the poor and to hand out tracts; he was known as "The Boy Preacher."

His next six years were eventful. He preached his first sermon at the age of sixteen. At age eighteen, he became the pastor of Waterbeach Baptist Chapel, preaching in a barn. Spurgeon preached over six hundred times before he reached the age of twenty. By 1854, he was well-known and was asked to become the pastor of New Park Street Chapel in London. In 1856, Spurgeon married Susannah Thompson; they had twin sons, both of whom later entered the ministry.

Spurgeon's compelling sermons and lively preaching style drew multitudes of people, and many came to Christ. Soon, the crowds had grown so large that they blocked the narrow streets near the church. Services eventually had to be held in rented halls, and he often preached to congregations of more than ten thousand. The Metropolitan Tabernacle was built in 1861 to accommodate the large numbers of people.

Spurgeon published over thirty-five hundred sermons, which were so popular that they sold by the ton. At one point, his sermons sold twenty-five thousand copies every week. The prime minister of England, members of the royal family, and Florence Nightingale, among others, went to hear him preach. Spurgeon preached to an estimated ten million people throughout his life. Not surprisingly, he is called the "Prince of Preachers."

In addition to his powerful preaching, Spurgeon founded and supported charitable outreaches, including educational institutions. His pastors' college, which is still in existence today, taught nearly nine hundred students in Spurgeon's time. He also founded the famous Stockwell Orphanage.

Charles Spurgeon died in 1892, and his death was mourned by many.

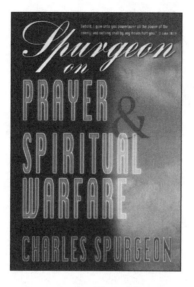

Spurgeon on Prayer and Spiritual Warfare
Charles H. Spurgeon

Here is a beloved treasury of six of Charles
Spurgeon's best-selling books. Many keys to living
a successful Christian life can be found in these
practical yet anointed words—keys to praying,
praising, and warring against Satan. Victory in Christ
can be yours as you implement these vital truths.
Answered prayers and a deeper faith in God await
you, so what are you waiting for?

ISBN: 978-0-88368-527-3 • Trade • 576 pages

WHITAKER
HOUSE
www.whitakerhouse.com

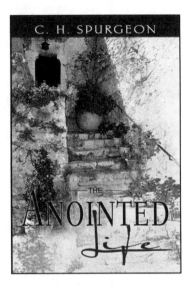

The Anointed Life
Charles H. Spurgeon

With a compassionate heart, Charles Spurgeon addresses
your doubts, fears, and questions about salvation, faith, and
how to live a life that pleases God. In a compelling blend
of down-to-earth common sense and heavenly wisdom,
he explains the great truths of forgiveness, redemption,
and power for living *The Anointed Life* in Christ. Once
you understand these truths, you can move forward with
confidence and serve God with true joy. Come—renew
your faith, enrich your spirit, and empower your life!

ISBN: 978-0-88368-473-3 • Trade • 624 pages

www.whitakerhouse.com

Grace and Power
Charles H. Spurgeon

Do you long to become the person God wants you to be? Do you wish you had more spiritual power? You can experience victory over sin, forgiveness and freedom from guilt, and a positive understanding of your salvation. Here is a dynamic collection of six of Charles Spurgeon's books, filled with biblical insights that will transform your life. It is possible to trade your weakness for God's strength and power—by His grace!

ISBN: 978-0-88368-589-1 • Trade • 624 pages

WHITAKER
HOUSE
www.whitakerhouse.com

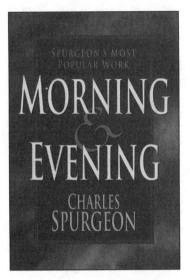

**Morning and Evening
(revised edition)**
Charles H. Spurgeon

"Encouraging thoughts are like honey to the heart," says Spurgeon, whose uplifting messages for each day of the year will bring comfort and refreshment to your walk with God. Whether you spend your time alone with God in the morning or the evening, or both, Spurgeon's message will powerfully affect your life, inspire your faith, and fill your heart with a profound sense of peace and joy.

ISBN: 978-0-88368-749-9 • Trade • 752 pages

www.whitakerhouse.com